Your
Developing
Baby

A Practical Handbook for
Parents of Baby's First Year

Dr. Kristin Lien Selvaag

BALBOA.PRESS
A DIVISION OF HAY HOUSE

Balboa Press books may be ordered through booksellers or by contacting:

Balboa Press
A Division of Hay House
1663 Liberty Drive
Bloomington, IN 47403
www.balboapress.com
1 (877) 407-4847

Because of the dynamic nature of the Internet, any web addresses or links contained in this book may have changed since publication and may no longer be valid. The views expressed in this work are solely those of the author and do not necessarily reflect the views of the publisher, and the publisher hereby disclaims any responsibility for them.

The author of this book does not dispense medical advice or prescribe the use of any technique as a form of treatment for physical, emotional, or medical problems without the advice of a physician, either directly or indirectly. The intent of the author is only to offer information of a general nature to help you in your quest for emotional and spiritual well-being. In the event you use any of the information in this book for yourself, which is your constitutional right, the author and the publisher assume no responsibility for your actions.

Any people depicted in stock imagery provided by Getty Images are models, and such images are being used for illustrative purposes only.
Certain stock imagery © Getty Images.

Interior Image Credit: Silje Ensby

Print information available on the last page.

ISBN: 978-1-9822-4532-0 (sc)
ISBN: 978-1-9822-4533-7 (e)

Balboa Press rev. date: 04/03/2020

CONTENTS

Babies are such a nice way to start people.
–Don Herold

FOREWORD

Modern human life is a flurry of speed, information overload, and noise. Technological developments have made us more mobile, yet we move less. We communicate more than ever but have less physical contact. Interpersonal presence has become a scarce resource. Consequently, many people are experiencing psychosomatic health issues, relating to the interaction of the mind and body. Increasingly younger children are experiencing this, even infants.

Parents of toddlers live hectic lives. Although parents in Norway are fortunate to have long parental leaves, parents are offered a plethora of baby-related activities that they often feel obliged to attend, filling up their days. The activities are usually beneficial for the child, but they often cause a lot of unnecessary and negative stress for both parents and children. Babies need the opposite of what modern life offers. Infants and babies have more than enough on their hands, just growing and developing. Their greatest need is mindful attention from their parents and siblings.

The most basic human psychological need is to be seen. Touch is an essential part of interpersonal communication, and it is especially important at the beginning of life before language is learned. Touch is crucial for connecting with your baby, getting to know each other's rhythm, and creating a mutually trusting relationship. Mutual understanding between parents and children is required to create a harmonious relationship, and it can eliminate a lot of the insecurities many new parents feel.

Baby massage can be an effective tool for creating early bonds between parents and children. The one performing the massage must calm down and mindfully focus on the baby to establish contact and get attuned to the baby's activity level. Baby massage also has a positive physical effect on the person performing the massage. Because babies live life at a slower pace, the child will have a calming effect on the adult when the baby massage is performed with mindful attention.

I have personally experienced the benefits of Kristin Lien Selvaag's "Baby Development and -Massage – the magic of touch with positive intention" classes. I participated with our youngest daughter, who was suffering from colic at the time. The problem gradually decreased with belly massage several times daily, as described in the book. Not only was her intestinal pain relieved, but she also felt more at ease and had less trouble sleeping. Massage is still – eight years later – the most effective help we can give, if she has problems falling asleep. Now, however, she asks for it when she needs to calm down or just wants to cuddle and be with us. She has also become skilled at massaging, and she spontaneously offers massages to her parents, her older sister, and her friends.

Baby massage is a way of being present with your child, which greatly benefits both the child and the parents. It can be done anywhere and requires very little equipment and organization. Learning well-proven techniques can thus be an investment that benefits the whole family.

Karen Kollien Nygaard
Psychologist, yoga og mindfulness teacher
www.kolliennygaard.no

PREFACE

Interacting playfully with your baby including baby massage, fun exercises and singing songs are great activities you can engage in with your newborn baby, which also provide great health benefits, for both of you.

Babies are so delightfully sweet and present, yet they are constantly developing from one stage to the next. I have always enjoyed spending time with children. I have three wonderful children myself, that I love and adore as well as they constantly challenge me and my husband.

In recent years, there has been an increasing interest in baby massage, playful engaging and stimulation exercises that promotes physical and mental development. Perhaps this is related to a greater awareness of the value of actively interacting with the little one. In Norway, we are privileged, as both mom and dad can take long parental leave. This is unique in a global context and it gives us a golden opportunity to develop a close bond with our baby.

Baby stimulation- and massage is a wonderful way to take part in your baby's development and to get acquainted with your baby and its body language. Skin-to-skin contact between parents and child is highly beneficial for your baby's emotional, muscular, skeletal and neurological development. To be touched with loving and confident hands is a very powerful language that will have a lasting impact.

In our increasingly digitalized environment, children grow up with parents constantly looking at a smartphone or a tablet. In doing so they appear withdrawn and distant. When did the smartphone become more important than the people around us? Setting time aside for being mindfully present through an activity like baby stimulation or – massage, interacting and playing with your baby, helps us to connect with our child. All the baby wants is you and your positive attention.

In my clinical practice as a chiropractor, many of my patients are babies that have various ailments and conditions. An important part of the treatment is intervention through touch and massage, or other techniques that I teach parents how to carry out at home. When the child is not feeling well the parents feel empowered when they can do something hands-on. The techniques parents practice at home will have a therapeutic effect. Although the techniques are not a substitute for the treatment I preform it still has an effect in stimulating the baby's body, coordination, and overall development.

Over the years, I have observed the benefits participants – children as well as parents – obtain from my classes. The class "Baby Development and -Massage – the magic of touch with positive intention" that I teach every Wednesday. With this book I hope to inspire you and assist you in understanding the child's developmental potential and how you best can promote the aid the development of your baby's muscles, skeleton, coordination and senses. You are the most important person in your child's life and there is nothing she wants more than to be with you! During play and massage you can feel each other's energy and explore each other's signals and interaction. The magic of touch is all about indulging in one another while building a trusting relationship and becoming acquainted through laughter and wonder.

In this book you will find a detailed guide and thorough descriptions of all maneuvers, exercises and strokes followed by illustrations, photos, songs, nursery rhymes and playful activities that promote and enhance the baby's overall development.

"He" and "She" is used in every other chapter to describe the child.

I am so grateful for your interest and desire to explore. Your baby is lucky – but so are you! Through these activities your relationship will positively impact the whole family for years to come, and it will provide a solid foundation for the rest of your child's life.

Dr. Kristin Lien Selvaag

"What you teach your children, you also teach their children."

In gratitude, Josefine, Nikolas, Lukas and Olav.
Thank you. You mean the world to me.
With love,
Always.

INTRODUCTION

Congratulations with your new baby! This is a special time to embrace, enjoy and get to know the little person who suddenly has become the most important part of your life.

It's a time of challenge. Not all children are born healthy and some are born too early. Parents may experience this time as exhausting, demanding and difficult due to lack of sleep and demands having a small baby may bring. It is not unusual to cry or have dark thoughts. Some also experience postnatal depression. Health professionals are observant to identify parents at risk and they offer additional support and assistance where needed.

Touch is fundamental for parents to attach to their baby and baby massage can be an effective way to ease problems associated with postnatal depression.

The uterus provides perfect temperature, lighting, soothing, smooth and muffled sounds, gentle, rocking movements and the right combination and amount of nutrients. Birthing is physically stressful. In addition, bright lights, colder temperatures, and sharp, loud sounds is a new situation. Massaging your baby is a great way to begin life outside the womb in a gentle and safe manner.

1
YOUR DEVELOPING BABY

"Babies are not things to be molded, but are people to be unfolded."

Why is touch important?

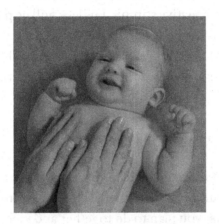

A child is constantly on his way towards the next developmental stage. Children have so much energy and are basically positive and genuine in everything they do. Small babies constantly experience a sense of empowerment. When they meet challenges, instead of feeling disappointed or powerless, they simply find other ways to tackle. They constantly use all their senses and never give up. Babies are limitless. They are also impressionable and, as parents, we can help them by giving them proper and focused stimulation as well as being positive role models who are calm, confident and secure.

Massage is "loving touch" of the skin which is the body's largest (sensory) organ. The massage involves stimulating all the senses. I always encourage parents to massage "with positive intention" meaning to be in touch with your heart while you massage. Through respectful and loving touch, you and your baby create a loving bond.

Everyone enjoys skin contact and it is especially important for infants at the beginning of life outside the womb. Babies like to be touched, lulled, held and feel cared for by a person close to them. By touching your baby in a respectful and loving manner you will get better at understanding your baby's body language, and you will gain mutual trust and respect for each other. Your baby will gain awareness about his own body and learn that he is important and valuable and he will better understand you as well. It's all in your touch.

Massage is a message of love from mom and dad to the baby. A variety of positive reactions occur in the body because of this joyful experience that has a positive and definite intention. All touch with positive intention has a beneficial effect on health. Mom and dad also get a boost of happiness and relaxation hormones that has a positive impact on body and mind. If the intention is not honest or you are not mentally present, it will be perceived as such. Your baby may turn away from this negative stimuli. His legs will be pulled up against the belly, his arms will be retracted towards the body and he will look in another direction and sometimes cry. We know that our intention is noticeable in terms of touch, body language and tone of voice, so put your heart into this precious time with your beautiful baby.

At what time can I start massaging my baby?

Immediately after birth. If your baby is healthy and the general condition is good, you can start by stroking the full body of your baby. Soon, you can gently begin massage routines. Tell your baby what you plan to do together and look for confirmation. You will see excitement and attentiveness in his or her gaze and body language.

We also know that when we are stressed the baby becomes stressed as well, worked up and uncooperative. This usually happens when we are in a rush and are unprepared. Try planning your days to avoid stressful situations. If you are both agitated and stressed you'd better stop and take a few deep breaths. Even if you are in a hurry please take a few slow, calming breaths to restore a sense of balance.

Think through the day ahead before going to bed, prepare and pack the diaper/changing bag. This will avoid stress on your way out the door the following day.

A positive interaction with your baby unfolds through repeated cuddling, rocking, lulling, massaging and vocal affirmations, signals to your baby that he is the most precious person in your world. These activities also strengthen the social part of the brain, located in the prefrontal cortex, the area of the brain right behind the eyes. It is especially receptive to care, touch, and encouragement from mom and dad during the first years of life.

In normal development, touch gives the baby a sense of security in himself, promotes a well-functioning social life, and helps the child understand the norms and rules of his culture. Parents show the way through positive action as we are not born with social knowledge. We depend on caregivers to teach us and we carry with us what we learn in the first years for the rest of our life.

Benefits of respectful touch and interaction with your baby

- Stimulates and regulates blood circulation. Blood vessels expand thus increasing the absorption of nutrients and oxygen and waste products are excreted from the body.

- Enhances production of oxytocin, serotonin and dopamine which promotes happiness, harmony and peace. The secretion of melatonin, a sleep-inducing hormone, increases with regular massage. The levels of the stress hormone cortisol decreases, which positively affect the immune system.

- Activates the nervous system, which has a beneficial effect on breathing patterns and heart rhythm, as well as promotes relaxation.

- Customized massage is beneficial for premature babies. Their body weight increases faster and they spend fewer days in the hospital. Please refer to you doctor or nurse for further instructions before preforming massage on your premature baby.

- Massage, play and interaction stimulate the communication between the left and right brain hemispheres, which strengthens coordination.

- During the massage and through interaction with parents the baby gets an understanding of his own body in relation to his surroundings.

- Regulates gastrointestinal functions that stimulates digestion. Baby massage can relieve abdominal pain and general indigestion and even painful symptoms of colic or irritable bowel syndrome.

- May reduce the duration of crying during the day.

- Aids the understanding of body language and nonverbal communication. Touch with positive intention is a form of communication.

- Loving touch with positive intention is a powerful language that is including, accepting and promotes intimacy. The baby feels accepted, loved and respected.

⊚ Promotes parents' sense of security and strengthens the natural bond between baby and parents, also known as the *parent-infant dyad*. They learn about their baby's limits and how their baby can be challenged and stimulated towards the next stage of development. It can help parents create a sense of security and harmony for their baby.

Bonding

Bonding is the attachment that develops between parents and their baby. The closeness parents feel towards the little one makes them want to shower the baby with love, affection, and warmth and protect and care for him even in the middle of the night when he cries.

Research shows that children who start their lives with a secure attachment bond to mom and dad or other primary caregivers – where they have been seen and heard – already as one-year-old functions better than their peers who have less secure relations. This first close relationship can cultivate a sense of security and positive self-esteem. Secure attachment bonds are very beneficial to the child growing up – strengthening socialization skills, general development, bonding to other people, as well as their empathy for and understanding of others. All in all, these bonds significantly affect their quality of life.

At 18 months of age, a securely attached child is less clingy and seeks less physical contact as he easily attunes with mom and dad. Attentive parents will encourage play and curiosity. A secure child with self-esteem understands both verbal and nonverbal communication from the caregiver.

All the activities, playful interaction and massage techniques in the book are ways to create healthy bonding.

Ways to encourage bonding:

- ⊚ Skin-to-skin contact via kangaroo technique "baby's naked chest touches parent's naked chest". It feels very safe and nurturing.
- ⊚ Eye-to-eye contact is the unspoken language. It feels very safe and nurturing.
- ⊚ Verbal communication though singing or talking about daily activities. The voice of the caregiver is the most soothing and comforting sound. The baby will try to imitate and vocalize sounds to communicate with you. Babies also enjoy listening to your conversations.

⊕ Cuddling and cradling, rocking your baby comfortably back and forth. It feels very safe, nurturing and including.

Skin

The skin covers the entire body and is our largest and most sensory sense organ. It protects us against the weather, wind, sun and microorganisms. The skin is waterproof and regulates temperature and it constantly processes new messages, unlike our eyes, ears and nose, which we can close against unwanted stimuli. The skin is always "on", receives everything, constantly and sends impulses to the brain.

The skin develops its sensitivity during the fetal stage. Scientists claim that 8 to 10-week-old fetuses in the womb responds to touch. Movement against the uterine wall are the first sensory experience.

Newborn babies can feel a difference between rough materials and soft, smooth fabrics. Research is increasingly showing that touch is essential for a person to develop both cognitively and physically. Animal experiments show that those who do not receive or experience touch, die or remain passive and helpless.

The skin accounts for about 18% of our body. It consists of skin cells, sweat glands, nerve endings, blood vessels and hair follicles. It is easy to understand the importance of touch since many processes are activated when a person is massaged. The brain perceives positive touch as a signal that causes the pituitary gland to release the "happiness" hormones, serotonin and dopamine, into the body through the blood. At the same time the adrenal glands reduce their production of cortisol and other stress-stimulating hormones, promoting our well-being. This strengthens our immune system and can contribute to better health.

Reflexes

A reflex is an involuntary motor response to a sensory stimulus. The function of the first reflexes is to give an experience of movement within the uterus. The reflexes help your baby actively engage in the birth process and ensure that he can take in food by searching and sucking from the breast or bottle. In addition, in the first months after birth, the reflexes assist the baby in turning his head to breathe and reaching out for mom and dad if he feels threatened. As the baby grows, develops and gains new skills, the first primitive reflexes will fade and disappear completely at 2 to 6 months of age.

Initially all movements seem uncoordinated and clumsy and gradually the movements become more controlled as the child develop movements, experience and muscle strength.

Examples of primitive reflexes

- The rooting and sucking reflexes are activated when you stroke your baby's cheek. The baby will automatically turn his head in the same direction, open his mouth and search for food and suck milk from the breast or bottle. This will be a willful act after approximately three months.

- The Moro reflex is provoked when the baby is scared or perceives a threat. It could be a loud sound, an unexpected or sudden touch, the feeling of falling or of losing balance. The baby will first stretch out his arms then retract them and sometimes cry. The fact that the baby extends his arms for an embrace while the head tilts backwards indicates that he is trying to cling to the caregiver in the moment of danger or threat.

- The palmar grasp reflex is provoked by stimuli or pressure in the palm of the baby's hand. The fingers cling to the stimuli, like your finger, with a healthy grip.

- The plantar reflex activates when stroking the soles of the foot. Toes spread and stretch out.

- The walking or stepping reflex is triggered when the soles of the baby's feet touch a surface. He will raise his foot and then the other. The stepping reflex is an important part of his development, preparing him to walk in the future.

- The crawling reflex is stimulated when the newborn baby is placed on his stomach. The legs will draw up and arms will retract, as if the baby wants to crawl. The blanket the baby is on will curl up.

- Asymmetrical tonic neck reflex is an important reflex in the birth process and during approximately the first six months after birth. It is activated when the head turns to the side. The arm and leg on the side the head is turned to extend in the same direction. The opposite arm and leg are bent.

Hormones

Hormones are the body's chemical messengers that are produced in certain glands of the body and transported through the blood. The word *hormone* is a Greek verb meaning "to set in motion," referring to the fact that each hormone excites or stimulates a particular part of the body or "target" gland. The stimulation is done automatically by our nervous system and is beyond our conscious control. Hormones regulate digestion, metabolism, respiration, tissue function, sensory perception, excretion, sleep, stress, growth and development, reproduction, movement and mood.

What we can control or influence ourselves, however, is our own mood. By being positive and present, we increase the production of hormones that are associated with positive moods – like oxytocin, serotonin, and dopamine – which are released into the bloodstream. While being stressed and sad cortisol and adrenalin is released into the blood stream wanting us to flee.

This is just one reason why massaging the baby should be part of the daily baby care routine. It promotes health both in the baby and in the parents. All involved become relaxed and peaceful.

An example of hormone secretion is when the lactating mother sees her baby showing signs of hunger, or she thinks her baby is hungry, the brain will send a message to the pituitary gland and breast milk will be excreted from the breast. The hormone oxytocin will be released from the pituitary gland and transported via the blood to the mammary gland. The milk ejection is released when the baby sucks the breast since the let-down reflex makes the breast milk flow. Some might experience a feeling of fullness and a tingling sensation in the breast.

When the milk is released from the breast, a sense of calm settles in both the mother and the baby because oxytocin – one of our happiness and well-being hormones – suppresses the production of another hormone, cortisol, which is produced in the adrenal glands. This creates a pleasant and relaxing feeling when the baby sucks milk from the breast. The body creates the conditions for making breastfeeding a positive and calming activity and experience for both of you.

Senses

During the baby massage all senses are challenged and stimulated.

- Eyes, ears, nose, mouth and skin.
- The nose and scent glands convert stimuli to perception of different scents.

- The mouth and taste buds perceive nuances like salt, sweet, sour, umami, and bitter taste.
- The skin and all nerve endings in the skin's different layers.

Throughout the massage, the baby will explore his taste buds, as the fingers and toes inserted into the mouth have a slight taste of oil from your skin. Baby's eyes observe what you do while listening to your voice singing or talking. The small, observant body feels your soft hands against his skin. All the senses are working while you are enjoying each other.

> Affection, familiarity and understanding may be created during eye contact.

Sight

A newborn baby does not have fully developed vision. He sees best from some distance, preferring round objects over square. It may relate to the fact that faces, which the baby thinks are most interesting, have a round, soft shape. You have probably noticed that the baby looks straight at you with wonder, interest or delight. The baby sees best from a distance of around 8–12 inches (20–30 cm). That is the distance to the mother's face when the baby is breastfeeding. From 3 months the baby can follow a moving toy or rattle. Around 4 to 7 months the baby can distinguish between colors. A new dimension of vision arises at around 6 months, when the baby develops perception of depth and distance. This is not a coincidence but a natural development and an evolutionary adaptation since the child in this developmental stage moves more freely by pulling himself by the arms or starting to crawl.

> A baby mobile, with different shapes and colors, is useful for sensory stimulation.

Hearing

Already during gestation, from weeks 20 to 24, the fetus can perceive and react to sounds from the world outside the womb. Mom's heartbeat and voice have been with the baby from the very first moment. This particular sound creates safety and calms the baby after birth. Dad's voice will also be familiar and safe for a baby who has heard his voice while in the womb and immediately after birth. The hearing develops further after birth by perceiving sounds and voices. This is necessary for language development.

The baby senses the secure and caring expression in his parents' voices, even though he does not understand the words yet. He can differentiate between the moods underlying the tone of voice when he gets praise or is negatively addressed. In the first phase of cooing all babies around the world "speak" identically; they have the same phonetic pattern of speech (speech sounds). It is fascinating that we all have a common language at the beginning of life.

At 4 to 6 months, hearing begins to affect the speech further and at 6 months the baby begins to become aware and interested in his own voice and "speaks" even more.

Sense of smell

Olfaction, or the sense of smell, is one of our earliest developed senses. Children's sense of smell is strong and the baby recognizes his mom's scent and prefers it to that of others. There have been studies on scent done with breast pads used by different mothers. The baby will turn towards his own mom's scent.

Try not to disturb the "smell image" the baby has of you by using perfume or aftershave. Your body emits chemical compounds perceived as smell. If the scent differs from one day to the next it may make the baby feel insecure. Remember that the best scent for you is your baby – and vice versa: your personal scent is your baby's favorite.

Taste

The sense of taste develops in the fetus in week 21. A newborn will be able to taste the difference between sweet, salty, bitter, sour and umami. A baby prefers sweet and umami, like that of breast milk. Babies will put things in their mouth, this sensory stimulation will develop their sense of taste.

All senses are important by themselves but also the interplay between the senses and the central nervous system is significant. It is an impressive and a complicated symphony of messages and signals that go back and forth via neural pathways. It is important to exercise all the senses so they will develop to their full potential. After all, our senses form the basis for how we perceive ourselves, our thoughts, feelings, our memory and learning.

Different developmental paths

Remember that all babies are different and have different developmental trajectories. We tend to focus on how things should or should not be done, what is right and what is optimal. We compare our own baby with others of the same age and we become uncertain and wonder why the babies develop differently.

"Why does not my daughter turn around like Emma? Emma can already turn around, and she is lying in a perfect position on her stomach, supporting her body with her elbows, ideally. Why doesn't my daughter do that? What have I done wrong? What can I do to improve? How can I help my baby to have a straighter body or be more cooperative?" These are some very common thoughts parents have because we are scanning for mistakes and problems. It is a way to justify our uncertainty and we soon end up becoming even more insecure than we were before we began comparing.

Everyone has these thoughts from time to time. But some engage in this kind of thinking more than others. We all want the same things: the best for our children and for ourselves. Seen from an evolutionary point of view it is a natural desire and a need for the family line to progress – strong and resilient – adapted to society and the environment.

By massaging and engaging in your baby regularly you will more easily realize the uniqueness of your own child as well as his reactions and patterns. We must accept that we are all different with varying temperaments and personalities. Each baby's development is uneven – at times slow, other times fast. It is quite okay that we are different and respect differences because we complement each other and thus society will develop. If you are uncertain about your baby's development and see signs of stagnation or if the baby does not develop as expected you should consult your healthcare provider.

A lovely baby was born last night
Giving life new meaning
and the world a precious new delight.

Unknown

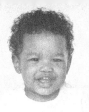

2

BABY MASSAGE AND POSITIVE INTERPLAY

"The importance of nurturing touch as well as a secure loving environment is well documented and aids in the healthy growth and maturation in children."

Communication

It is an important part of the positive interplay that the baby can express her "opinion" about the interaction. Communication in the infant phase is non-verbal, but recognizing the subtle cues of acceptance or rejection is not difficult. As parents, we listen and perceive body language and other signals that she tries to send. A baby who wants to be touched will remain calm and have a relaxed body, smile and be full of joy when she sees that you are preparing, for example warming the oil between the palms of your hands, telling her what you plan to do. It is ok to proceed if she "answers" with excitement and attentiveness.

A baby who does not want a massage or to be touched becomes restless and turns away rejecting your hands when you ask or prepare to massage her. Stop, wait and try again, maybe later is a better time for your baby. This is where the interplay begins and her boundaries and limits are respected.

Find the right time for positive interplay and massage

You may massage your baby anytime of the day when she "answers" with excitement and attentiveness. However, there are certain times of the day that are more approachable. For example, when she is more receptive, awake and calm, set aside time together.

These phases are (day and night):

- Sleep (deep- and light sleep)
- Drowsy
- Crying

- Active state of wakefulness
- **Quiet state of wakefulness – is the best time to massage!**

When the baby is sleepy or drowsy she wants to be left alone, just like us adults. Light stroking across the face from forehead down along the nose may be calming and can help the baby fall asleep if she is a little restless. These light and soft touches can recreate the feeling of safety when lying on mom's or dad's chest.

When the baby is not at ease or is crying it is better to comfort her in your arms. Find out why she is feeling uneasy, hungry, afraid, wet or tired? A light stroke with your palm across her back and lulling her in your safe embrace while you talk soothingly or sing, may do the trick. When she is unhappy or crying she needs to feel safe more than she needs a massage.

In the phase of active wakefulness the baby's attention is focused on what is happening around her. In a situation where dad or mom may come home from work or siblings express attention and wanting to play is not the best time for a massage. The active awake phase is absorbed by things that happen in her immediate surroundings. She gets involved with what is happening around her and may not want to lie still and have a massage.

The best time to do baby massage is in the calm awake phase. In this phase she is receptive for quality time with you. You can also recognize this phase as the time when she may lie by herself and coo, comfortable in her own company.

Preparation

The most important thing is that you are present and mindful together with your baby. Nevertheless, it may be useful to have a few things available to make it more enjoyable for both of you:

- Set aside 10–20 minutes.
- Ensure an even temperature in the room, 68–77 degrees Fahrenheit (20–25 degrees Celsius) is optimal.
- Find a safe and secure place, preferably on the floor, so that the child can move freely and without you worrying about her getting hurt, risking a fall from a height or rubbing against sharp edges of furniture.

- Use a plastic underlay that can withstand oil and spillage. You may also use a suitable protective mattress, disposable paper, washable plastic sheets or a padded changing mat.
- Towels to lie on and to clean up.
- It is also advisable to use a soft blanket to cradle the head of a newborn baby can feel reassuring.
- Make your own oil for the massage. Pure without parabens, equal amounts of ecological extra virgin cold pressed olive oil and sunflower oil.

You might like to include:

- Quiet music creates harmony and provides a pleasant mood and ambience in the room.
- It may be useful to have a toy or a rattle to divert attention from the massage.
- Diapers and clothes to change into should be ready, or pajamas, if you choose to do the massage after the evening bath.
- Everything you need should be ready and within reach, so you can avoid leaving the baby alone during the playful interaction.

Massage oil

The baby's skin is sensitive and very soft and feels like silk. Through regular massage with the appropriate oil, the dead skin cells will be washed away and the blood circulation is stimulated and gives the skin a fresh glow. Using oil during the massage allows your hands to slide with ease over the skin and the skin will not be uncomfortably stretched. The oil should be even and fine, not sticky, thick or oily. The baby tends to put hands and feet in her mouth so the oil must be of good quality and without additives and preservatives.

You can make the very best massage oil from products you have on your kitchen counter. Use organic cold-pressed extra virgin olive oil mixed with an equal amount of sunflower oil of good quality. This mixture has a mild scent and the texture is suitable for lubricating the fine skin. Olive oil is slightly viscous and sunflower oil has a thinner consistency with a neutral scent and is more easily absorbed. Mix this together in a bottle and shake well. The mixture is safe to apply on delicate skin, easy to make and cheap, and you probably have them on your kitchen counter. In addition this oil mixture is full of vitamins and minerals that absorbs well and are beneficial for the fine skin. You may use it in the bath to prevent dry skin or use it on dry crusts on scalp.

- Use a paraben-free plastic bottle for the oil mixture. The baby can hold the bottle and, in this way, participate in the massage. After a while she will recognize the bottle and rejoice anticipating for what is coming – a good time with you.
- If you pour out too much oil into your hands, do not pour it back into the bottle since it can contaminate the contents of the bottle having been out already. Apply the excess elsewhere on the baby or wipe the residue on a towel.
- Remove jewelry that can get in the way or scratch the fine, delicate skin of your baby. Also, keep the phone in silent mode or turn it off completely. This lovely moment is dedicated to the two of you and is best enjoyed without unnecessary disturbances.
- If you want to buy baby massage oil you can find many options in a health food store.
- Pay attention and be careful with products that you apply on the baby's skin and try to use only natural and organic products.
- If the oil is natural and organic, just wipe of the excess oil with a towel. If the oil contains parabens or minerals, it should be washed off right after the massage.

Massage

How much pressure can I apply?

A newborn baby cannot tolerate as much pressure on the body as a baby who is a few months older and has developed more muscle mass. A baby develops more muscles when she starts moving around, at which time you may apply a little more pressure to the small body.

When you apply pressure to the muscles, nerve connections to the brain are connected between the body and the brain. With repetitive stimuli like massage, play, activity and movement the baby will develop an understanding of her own body. Eventually, she will also understand that she can choose her own movements – that she can decide and carry out the action herself. It could be grabbing the rattle that is beside the blanket, rolling the ball across the floor or touching her own reflection in a mirror. All these acts of self-determination leave the baby feeling empowered.

What should I do if my baby does not like to be massaged?

Almost everyone like a massage. Try to find out which needs your baby has if she cries or turns away from you during your session. Is she hungry, tired, or in need of something else?

I recommend that you find the quiet and wakeful state, see page 14, when your baby is more receptive to your interaction and massage. Tell your baby what you plan to do before you start and do not proceede if she is not in receptive mood.

When you introduce massage for the first time, start by massaging the feet and proceed to other parts of the body as she gets used to the strokes.

When should I not massage my baby?

In case of illness, fever, malaise, skin infection, or after vaccination, when the area may be tender and sore. Consult your healthcare professional if you are unsure.

Now you can start

Communicate with your baby and ask for permission to massage and consider your baby's body language. If the signals are positive you can prepare for a massage based on the tips on page 14. Start by taking a few deep breaths. This will put you in a good, peaceful mood and prepares you for the joyful, tranquil moments ahead. Also, you may stretch your arms above your head and bend your upper body to each side, feeling the stretch along the side of the chest. Then wave your fingers over your baby's face to get her attention. Eventually she realizes what you are doing and understands what is coming – a wonderful time with you!

It is not necessary to do these stretches but I recommend it because it is a great way to get in the right frame of mind for the massage and it puts you both in a good mood filled with anticipation. Your baby quickly learns to recognize your movements and the expectation of what is coming will fill her with joy.

Undress your baby, pour the oil into your hands and rub your palms together to warm the oil. Maintain eye contact. If she responds with positive signals you may proceed and distribute the oil on her body.

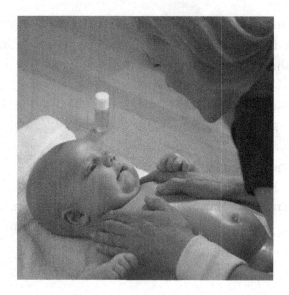

Preform the massage with secure and confident hands.

If the child wants to move or turn around while you have this playful interaction, you adjust yourself and the strokes accordingly.

Massaging different parts of the body

Some days you just have time to massage a small part of the body and other days you can run through an entire program. This chapter describes how each part of the body can be massaged.

When you perform massage on your baby for the first time it is wise to begin with the legs and feet. It is a good place to ease into the massage since it demands the least commitment on the baby's behalf. It is the part furthest away from the core of the body. You can follow the order as described on the following pages of the book, until the child is used to the massage and you can surprise and challenge her by massaging areas that she is unaccustomed to. All steps can be repeated 5–6 times on each body part, but the number of repetitions may vary according to the time and her mood. You can assess as you go along and adjust to your baby.

Many of the exercises have been given a name so that you can play with the meaning of the word throughout the massage. Other exercises can be combined with a nursery rhyme. For example, "waterfall," which is focused on the belly. There are many opportunities to talk about what a waterfall is and the sensational sounds it makes. Let your imagination run free and go on an exploration.

Remember that your light and safe handling of your baby with your hands is perfect for her. There is no perfect "stroke," "method," or "direction" – your respect and positive intention shines through in your strokes and will be experienced as such.

How often should I massage?

Anywhere from every day to a few times a week. Do not feel guilty if you do not do it as often as you want – all touch with positive intention is good and beneficial. Just be mindful when you are together and stroke, touch and sing as often as you can.

How long can I massage?

From a few minutes, up to 20 minutes is ideal. After 20 minutes, the baby often loses interest. Explore and find your baby's ideal tolerance.

Can I do something wrong?

As long as the intention is positive and you adjust pressure according to the baby's development, you can do no wrong with a healthy child.

Legs

Babies love to get their legs massaged. It stimulates blood circulation and muscle development.

Heat the oil between the palms of your hands and distribute on your baby's one leg.

1. The C-grip. Form your hand like a C. Hold around your baby's thigh, near the groin, and sweep down the thigh in a calm movement, over the knee, leg, ankle, and toes. Switch hands and do the same motion on the other side of the leg.

2. Squeeze and slide. Place both hands on your baby's thigh. Press lightly on the thigh muscles until you feel resistance in the muscle, release and without losing skin contact, slide calmly down towards the lower leg. Squeeze the calf and slide down to the ankle.

Perform the same routine on the other leg. Tell your baby that you will now continue with the other leg.

All steps can be repeated 5-6 times on each leg.

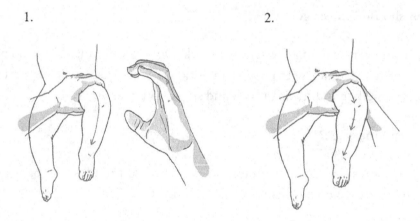

1.   2.

Feet and toes

The sole of the foot is sensitive due to its many nerve endings.

1. Stroke your thumbs against the soles of the feet alternately from heel to toe, while holding the ankle with two fingers to follow your baby's movements, without losing your stroke.

2. Small circles. Make small, circular movements with the tip of your thumb throughout the sole of the foot.

3. The Caterpillar. Crawl with your thumb like a caterpillar, from the heel to the toes. Repeat until you have thumb-crawled to each toe.

4. Massage toes. Grab the big toe with three fingers and rock it gently. Do the same motion with every toe.

All steps can be repeated 5-6 times on each foot.

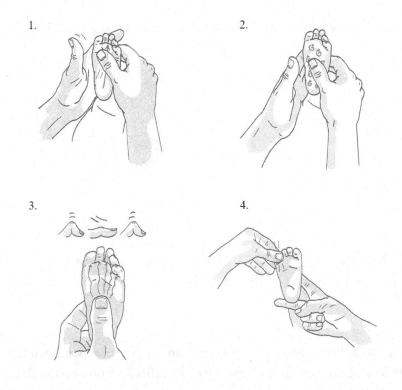

In the beginning the baby might curl his toes. Don't worry, let your baby get used to the strokes and everything will be fine.

Instep

Massaging the foot and instep is safe, feels good and increases the strength upwards the leg.

1. Place the foot in your hand and stroke the thumbs alternately from the top of the toes to the ankle.

2. With your thumbs, make a circular movement on each side of the ankle while the foot is resting in your hand.

3. Support the calf with the other hand and stroke with the palm of your hand from the toes and up the calf.

All steps can be repeated 5-6 times on each instep.

You can do this exercise when your baby is about to sleep; it has a soothing effect.

1.   2.   3.

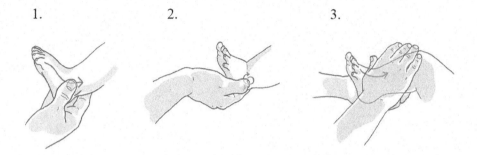

> All the strokes can be repeated 5–6 times. When you finish one leg and foot, continue the same exercises on the other leg.

> It is a good idea to tell your baby where you are in the process, what you are doing, and what you intend to do, for example "Now I finished this leg and will continue massaging your other leg."

Bottom

The baby lies on her back. Rest the back of her thighs in the bend between your thumb and index finger and stroke your hands over the buttock muscles. Make a circular motion around the buttocks, including the hips, pelvis, and the area between the pelvis and the lower back.

All steps can be repeated 5-6 times.

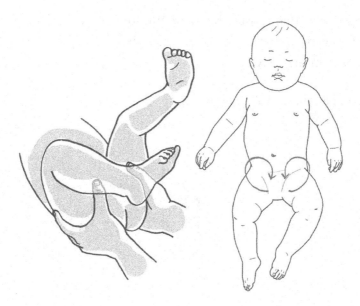

Belly

When you massage the belly, you are in fact also massaging the digestive organs. Do the movements in a clockwise direction; in this way you will be following the direction of the movement of the digestive system and may aid constipation.

1. The Waterfall. Use your palm to stroke from the bottom of the rib cage to the pelvic floor. Be gentle and feel the resistance of the baby's tummy; look at the reaction and adjust the pressure so that it is perceived as pleasant.

2. The Circle. Make a circle below the rib cage in clockwise direction.

3. The Arc. Make an arc below the rib cage, sweeping from the right hip to the left hip.

4. I Love You – this is a nice rhyme to use while massaging:

    *   I: Left side: Stroke down from the rib cage to the hip while saying "I Love You."
    *   L: Make an inverted L from baby's right side, below the rib cage, over to the left and straight down the hip while saying "I Love You."
    *   U: Make an arc from the baby's right hip to the left hip, while enthusiastically saying "I Love You."

This is an exercise that most babies and children enjoy. The active interaction with movement and appropriate words captivates children – they can really feel that they are taking part in the activity.

All steps can be repeated 5–6 times.

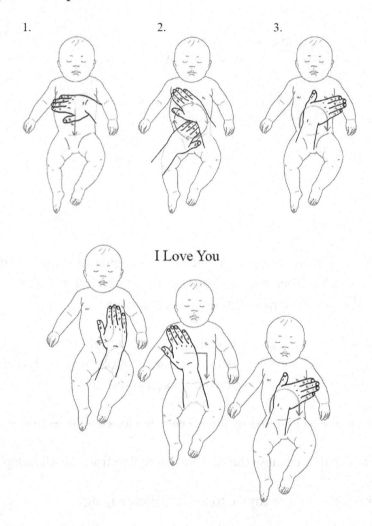

I Love You

All the tummy strokes should follow in a clockwise direction, in accordance with the digestive system.

Chest

Warm up the oil between your palms. Keep both palms on your baby's chest for about 5–10 seconds and feel her heartbeat. Send warmth from your heart via your hands to your baby's chest. Say some comforting words with your soft voice.

1. The Heart. Rest your hands on the middle of the chest for a few seconds. Calmly, and in a grounded manner, sweep up towards the shoulders. Gliding down the side of the body, collect your hands below the navel and stroke up to the starting point. The motion looks like the heart shape.

2. The Open Book. Rest your hands in the middle of your baby's chest for a few seconds before you sweep your hands out to the side, as if opening a book.

3. The X. Rest both hands on her chest for a few seconds before you sweep the right hand up to the left shoulder and back. Do the same with your left hand: sweep it up to the right shoulder and back to the starting point. Once you have gained more experience with this exercise, you can gently squeeze around the shoulder joint.

All steps can be repeated 5-6 times.

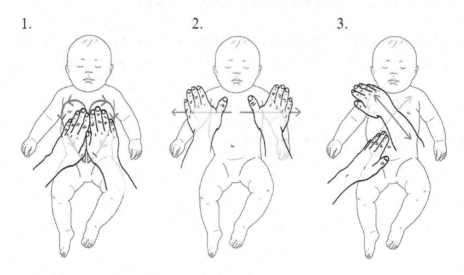

Arms

Heat the oil between the palms of your hands and distribute on your baby's one arm.

1. The C-grip. Form your hand like a C. Hold around the baby's arm at the armpit and sweep in a relaxed and gentle manner down over the elbow, forearm, hand and fingers. Alternate your hands.

2. Squeeze and slide. Place both hands on your baby's upper arm. Press lightly on the arm muscles until you feel resistance in the muscle, release, and without losing skin contact, slide calmly down to the forearm. Press lightly on the forearm and slide down to the fingers.

    Perform the same routine on the other arm. Tell your baby that you will now continue with the other arm.

All steps can be repeated 5-6 times on each arm.

Hands

1. Create circles inside your baby's palm with your thumb.

2. Massage your baby's fingers between your thumb and index finger. *«All are my favorite fingers»*, see page 64, is a fun nursery rhyme to use while massaging.

3. Stroke the back of the hand.

All steps can be repeated 5-6 times on each hand.

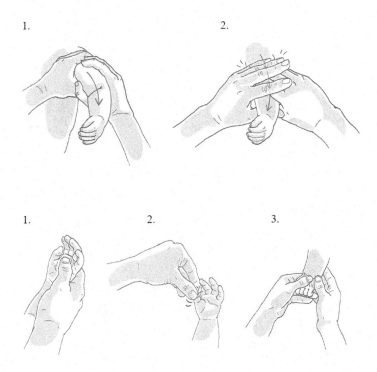

Back

Heat the oil between your palms and gently distribute it on the back.

1. The Waterfall A. Stroke with a flat palm from the neck towards the bottom; alternate hands.

2. The Fan. Hold both hands around the body, then stroke with the thumbs over the back muscles in a fanlike motion towards the neck. Then, slide the palms down towards the bottom and repeat.

3. The Pattern. On the muscles along the spine, draw patterns with your index and middle fingers (for example waves, figure 8, curls – be creative, try several and make your own).

4. Up and Down. Keep one hand on each side of the spine and stroke alternately up and down, firmly but gently. Move your hands in opposite directions.

5. The Waterfall B. Baby lies perpendicular to you. Support the bottom with one hand and, with the other, stroke down along the back.

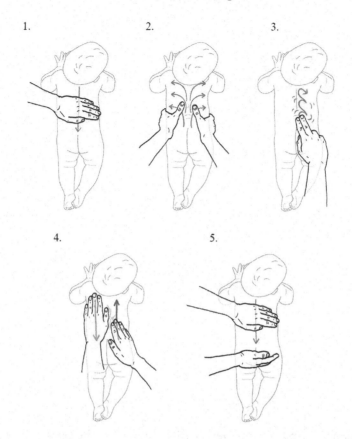

All steps can be repeated 5–6 times. All exercises can also be done when the baby is lying perpendicularly in front of you. Be flexible and adjust to the baby.

It is okay to stretch the skin, just make sure you apply enough oil so it feels pleasant.

Head and face

To be touched gently in the face is a pleasant feeling. We often do it on ourselves, as adults, massaging our temples and rubbing our eyes and forehead. There is no need to use oil in this sequence. All steps can be repeated 3–5 times. Always finish the massage with some cuddling. Say something that feels right for you to wind down the pleasurable time you had together, like: "Thank you, my love, for this nice wonderful heartfelt time we have together".

1. The Forehead. With flat palms stroke across his forehead, gently pulling to the side. Here you can add playful sentence: "Where is daddy/mommy? Here I am!" Slide hands to each side.

2. The Temples. Make circular movements on the temples and continue the circular movement towards the crown of the head, then slide your hands behind the ears, forward to the jawbone and under the chin.

3. The Eyebrows. With your thumbs, stroke the arc above the eyes (eyebrows), from the top of the nose to the outer corner of the eye.

4. The Eye Arc. With your thumbs, stroke the area below the eye, from the medial corner of the eye to the outer corner of the eye.

5. The Ears. Massage the ear cartilage and earlobes between your fingers.

The baby will not be able to maintain eye contact throughout any routine. It can be intense so she will need a break but will soon return your gaze. This is not a sign of rejection.

If you want your massage to have a more relaxing effect, you can end your arm and leg massage by stroking from the armpits to the hands and from the hips to the feet. If you do the strokes in the opposite direction, towards the core it will have an invigorating effect.

Full-body massage

Once you have received a positive sign and you have time for a full body massage, you may start stroking your hands from the head, down the length of the body, to the feet. Hold the soles of the feet against your palms and feel how receptive your baby is to the contact and interaction with you. Begin with leg massage. Then continue with the bottom, tummy, chest, arms, hands, back, and, finally, the head and face.

Holding your palms against the soles of the feet can be performed without a massage.

It feels good for your baby to be touched and stroked over the entire body, from the head and down to the feet. Get synchronized with your baby by placing your palms against the baby's chest for a few seconds, being fully present. Follow her movements – and enjoy the "dance" together. It is the start of a good interaction.

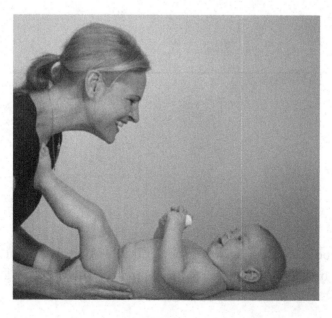

3

PLAYFUL EVERYDAY ROUTINES - AND A MESSAGE
TO DAD AND SIBLINGS

"What day is it?" asked Pooh. "It's today," squeaked Piglet. "My favourite day," said Pooh.

Involving dad and siblings

Important note to dad

The expectant father has not felt the growing baby inside his body. His way to prepare for life with a small baby has been entirely different from mom's. The first few weeks with the newborn baby, fathers may feel rejected, somewhat awkward and get frustrated. It's no wonder, since mom is breastfeeding, caring for, and seemingly inseparable from the baby during the first period after birth. Although she doesn't always manage to express the importance of dad's presence, it is essential that he is present and near. Dad is especially important if mom has had a difficult delivery or develops postnatal depression.

Dad can also be involved in the baby massage. He is important. His hands are perfect for the baby. Although it may seem daunting to suddenly get a small body placed in his lap, a massage routine with concrete and simple exercises can be a great tool getting to know the little child's body. In this way, dad is also included and a great help – there is a need for him and he does something positive and good for the baby while they develop their own unique bond.

When dad and the baby are engaged in the massage, they develop close ties in a caring and loving way, which is important for both. Dad will find that the baby loves the way he touches him and that he gets to know the little body in a exclusive and trusting manner. These moments of happiness are special for both of them, and they can make their own routine as they go along.

Note to dad:

Early bonding activities may include:

- Involve yourself in your partner's pregnancy and birth preparations.
- During the pregnancy read, talk, and sing together. The fetus at weeks 20-24 can hear your voice. Touch and stroke moms growing belly; it will become natural for you to continue with positive touch after the baby is born.
- During delivery, be active and support your partner.
- Change diapers and bottle-feed.
- Develop your own massage routines.
- Let your baby indulge in you – let him touch your face and feel how the texture differs from mom's – maybe you have a beard or mustache?
- Walk with the baby in a stroller or carry your baby in a sling or shawl safely secured to your chest.
- Participate in bedtime routines.

Program for dads

"His little hands stole my heart. His little feet ran away with it."

My experience is that dads quickly create their own routines – that only the two of them know.

These are suggestions to get you started.

1. The Heartbeat. Rest your hands on the middle of your baby's chest for a few seconds and feel the heart beats. Send your love through your hands to your baby.

2. The Heart. Rest your hands in the middle of the chest. Glide calmly up towards the shoulders. Glide down the side of the body, gather your hands below the navel, continue back to the chest, and repeat.

3. Bicycling. Let the baby's ankles rest in your palms. Alternately bend each knee up towards the baby's belly, while you carefully stretch the other leg, as if you are bicycling. Do the movements at a calm pace. Repeat 4–5 times.

4. Power pose stretch. Let your baby grasp your thumbs and stretch the arms out to each side. Cross the arms over the chest and stretch the arms out to each side again.

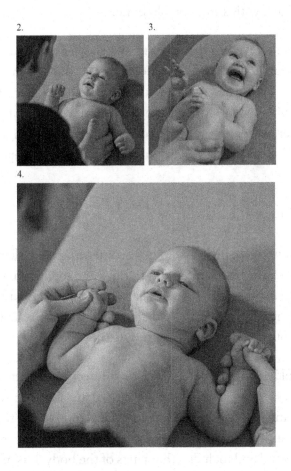

All exercises can be repeated 4-5 times.

Important note to siblings

Siblings-the definition that comprises love, strife, competition and forever friends.

Even if a sibling has been preparing for many months to be a big brother or big sister, and is really looking forward, a new sibling can create uncertainty. They want to help but do not know how. By including siblings in the baby massage, they will develop a close and strong bond. The big brother or big sister feels there is a use for them and that they can do something that their young sibling enjoys, and this makes them feel appreciated. This gives their relationship a solid foundation. They develop an amicable tone among themselves, that will last a lifetime. It is easier to be kind to someone to whom you feel you matter and who gives you positive feedback with smiles and laughter.

Dad or mom should be involved in this interaction, so that older siblings understand what kind of touch is comfortable and has the greatest impact. Start by introducing, for example, foot massage, which is simple, informal, and comfortable. The older siblings will feel useful, and the young siblings will love the attention they get. Eventually the touches can be enriched with more strokes, exercises, and games. Older siblings will gain an increasing sense of empowerment and self-confidence, which will have a positive impact in the new family situation.

Routines for older siblings

Try to let the time spent with the little one involve something the older siblings are interested in. It could be a fictional character, trains and cars, dolls and teddy bears, Legos, farm animals, and other games of the imagination. The older sibling can pretend that the figure comes crawling, sliding, walking or driving up the baby's legs and arms. They can also stroke the baby's body and talk about what happens in a movie they like.

My experience is that older siblings get excited to connect with their little sister or brother when parents use stories, songs, and rhymes that they are familiar with. *The Little Pig*, for instance, is a simple rhyme where they can have a playful interaction together. Massaging the feet or hands is another simple exercise that older siblings can engage in. As they get the hang of it, the routine can expand and include other parts of the body. It is important that you, as a parent, pay close attention to the interaction and guide the sibling in the beginning so that it becomes a positive experience. See chapter 5 for suggested songs and nursery rhymes.

Here are some suggestions for daily routines that are fun and stimulating. Tell your baby what you plan to do and observe his expressions and body language. With positive feedback, proceed with your plan. If he seems uncomfortable, wait and try the exercises again a little later. All exercises should be done with fun and joy; never force him into something he does not like.

Good morning, sweetheart

Are you ready for a new day with new challenges? You will now learn five great exercises that will give you both a lovely start to the day. Use this opportunity to enjoy your time with each other while you wake up together and start the day with positive intentions. Tell him what you plan to do, and say something like, "Good morning, my sweet little one, rise and shine!" Keep in mind and respect that your baby may need a little extra time to wake up and may only be ready for the challenge a little later.

The first three parts of the program can be done from the time your baby is newborn. You should wait to perform parts 4 and 5 until the baby is a few weeks old, or until he has strengthened his neck muscles and has better control of head movement.

If your baby is not ready for this playful awakening, you may engage him in a rhyme instead:

Cocks Crow
Cocks crow in the morn
　　To tell us to rise,
And he who lies late
　　Will never be wise.

For early to bed
　　And early to rise,
Is the way to be healthy
　　And wealthy and wise.

Parents can be inspired by children and stretch for a few seconds before we ourselves get out of bed: stretch your whole body with arms above the head.

When you stand up:

- stretch to each side.
- Swing your arms in big circles.
- Shrug your shoulders.
- Rotate your hips.

1. The Heart. Start your interaction by holding your hands on her chest and say some kind words. "Good morning, sweetheart, rise and shine!" Or anything that comes naturally to you. Hold for 10–15 seconds.

2. The Sun. Let your baby grasp your thumbs and make circles, gently rotating the baby's shoulders and elbow joints outwards and then inwards. Say a few words that come naturally to you, like, "Rise and shine with the sun." Repeat 4–5 times.

3. Bicycling. Let the baby's ankles rest in your palms. Alternately bend each knee up towards the baby's belly, while you carefully stretch the other leg, as if you are bicycling. Do the movements at a calm pace. Repeat 4–5 times.

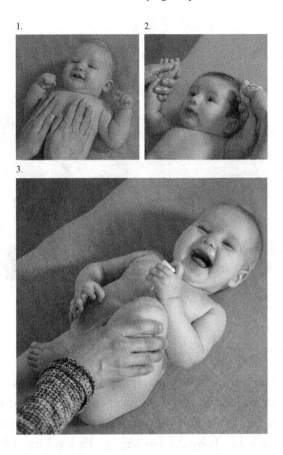

4. Stand up. Let your baby hold your thumbs while you hold around her forearms. Invite her to pull herself up. Once you can feel strength and resistance from her shoulders, she can pull herself up on her own initiative. To do this exercise, she must have strength in her neck. If the head hangs backward, the neck needs to be strengthened. Just like the belly position, this exercise is good practice to strengthen her neck, shoulders and torso. In the beginning it is enough to just feel the resistance of the shoulders and see that she is working on raising her head. Please note, that as the baby gets stronger, she will want to get up to a standing position, which is ok. It's a nice and fun exercise that gives your baby a sense of empowerment.

5. Geyser. Hold around your baby's chest and lift her up from a sitting or standing position, like a geyser, and say, "Good morning, my sunshine, what a wonderful beginning to our day! I can't wait to spend the morning with you!" Give a big hug. Your child will get a good, harmonious start to the day when you do this together. If you only have time for one or two of these exercises, it is still a great start of the day.

4.
5.

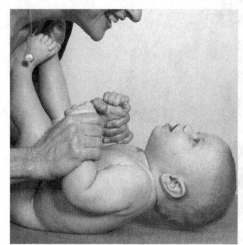

Superstar

This is a super exercise and a fun game that strengthens your harmonious interaction and helps your baby develop an understanding of himself and the world around him, among other things using gravity. This exercise has two levels: One level for the smaller babies who don't have the strength to lift their heads by themselves, and a level for babies who are able to lift their heads.

For the smaller babies:

1. Lie down on your back with your knees bent and your feet on the ground.
2. Place the baby on your shins, so that the baby's chin rests between your knees. Keep eye contact with your baby.
3. Lift your legs up to a 90-degree angle. The baby lies flat and level to the ground. Hold firmly around your baby's body.
4. Raise your legs a little higher, so the baby is lying with his head slightly down and feels gravity pulling in the opposite direction of what he is used to.
5. Lower your legs again, so the baby restores a normal sense of gravity. You can do this exercise of raising and lowering your legs several times. When the baby becomes restless or indicates that he has had enough, stop.

Superstars who are in control of their head movements:

1. Lie down on your back with your knees bent and your feet on the ground.
2. Place the baby on your shins. Keep eye contact through the exercise, and throughout the exercise assess whether your baby can handle the challenges. Hold firmly around your baby's body.
3. Lift your legs up to a 90-degree angle. The baby lies flat and level to the ground.
4. Raise one leg a little, so that the baby will be slightly tilted. This will automatically induce your baby to attempt to stabilize himself using muscles from the opposite arm and leg, and this helps strengthen his back muscles.
5. Raise both your legs a little higher, so the baby is lying with his head slightly down and feels gravity pulling in the opposite direction of what he is used to.
6. Take a good grip around the baby's chest, lift him up, and let him slide down your shins, ending in a sitting position on your stomach. In this position, you can have a nice conversation or sing a happy song.

Be aware of your baby's need for a break.

Good night

After a day filled with play, interaction and daily routines, it is good for your baby to calm down. Small children have all their senses wide open and are continuously processing new information all day. Here you will learn some good exercises that will leave your baby calm after a long day and help him restore peace and balance in the body. It's okay to do the exercises with clothes or pajamas on as this is the last thing you do before bedtime. In exercises 1–5, the baby lies on his back. Conclude the exercises by stroking from the hip down towards the toes and from the armpit towards the fingers – it has a relaxing effect.

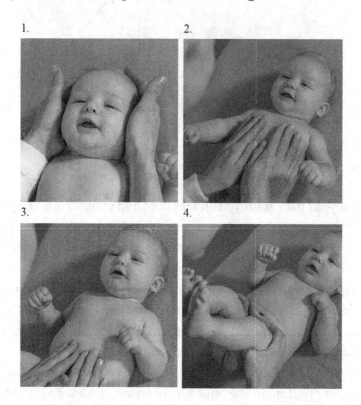

1. Head, shoulders, knees, and toes. Stroke from the head down along the body.

2. The Heartbeat. Rest your hands in the middle of your baby's chest for a few seconds. This is a good way to start the interaction. Say, "Good night, sweetheart, I love you so much," or anything else that comes to you.

3.   The Heart. Rest your hands on the middle of the chest for a few seconds. Glide up towards the shoulders, down along the side of the body, gather your hands below the navel, and return to the chest with your hands together. Hold your hands for a few seconds over his chest and feel the heartbeat. Repeat the exercise.

4.   The Screw. Hold the baby's thighs, knees together. Rotate legs with small movements in a clockwise fashion.

5.   6.

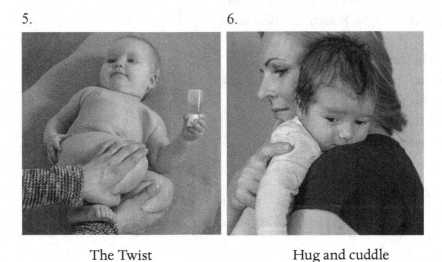

The Twist   Hug and cuddle

5.   The Twist. Hold the baby's thighs while calmly moving them gently to the right side, counting 1 2,3,4. Do the same on the left side.

6.   Hug and cuddle while you sing a song. Give your baby a last hug while you sing a peaceful lullaby. This is a nice ending to the day.

Lullabies for your Little Star

Twinkle, twinkle, little star
Twinkle, twinkle, little star,
How I wonder what you are!
Up above the world so high,
Like a diamond in the sky.

When the blazing sun is gone
When he nothing shines upon,
Then you show your little light,
Twinkle, twinkle, all the night.

Rock-a-Bye, Baby, on the treetop!
When the wind blows the cradle will rock,
When the bough breaks the cradle will fall.
Down will come baby, bough, cradle and all.

The Man in the Moon
The Man in the Moon looked out of the moon,
And this is what he said,
"'Tis time that, now I'm getting up,
All babies went to bed."

Good night, sweetheart, sleep and dream sweetly all night long. I look forward to seeing you up in the morning.

Getting started – a four-week program for touch, movement, development and coordination

This four-week program is perfect if you want some continuity in the massage and playful interaction and want to follow a regular schedule the next few weeks. We will delve into a different theme each week, and I recommend that you have a few days per week available for each theme. It is very enjoyable, and you quickly settle into a routine. Refer to page 14 for preparation and equipment.

Week 1: Touch

This first week is when you will get to know your baby's body. Make the necessary preparations and start massaging the legs before you progress to massage the chest, arms, and hands.

Babies love to get their legs massaged, it stimulates blood circulation and muscle development.

Respect your baby by asking for permission and telling him what you plan to do before you begin.

Legs

Heat the oil between the palms of your hands and distribute on your baby's one leg.

1. The C-grip. Form your hand like a C. Hold around your baby's thigh, near the groin, and sweep down the thigh in a calm movement, over the knee, leg, ankle, and toes. Switch hands and do the same motion on the other side of the leg.

2. Squeeze and slide. Place both hands on your baby's thigh. Press lightly on the thigh muscles until you feel resistance in the muscle, release and without losing skin contact, slide calmly down towards the lower leg. Squeeze the calf and slide down to the ankle.

Perform the same routine on the other leg. Tell your baby that you will now continue with the other leg.

All steps can be repeated 5-6 times on each leg.

1.   2.

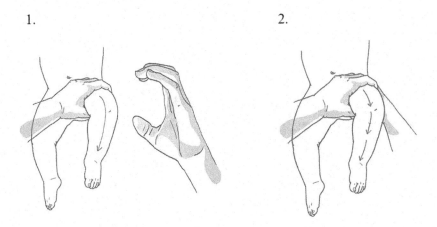

Feet and toes

1. Stroke your thumbs against the soles of the feet alternately from heel to toe, while holding the ankle with two fingers to follow your baby's movements, without losing your stroke.

2. Small circles. Make small, circular movements with the tip of your thumb throughout the sole of the foot.

3. The Caterpillar. Crawl with your thumb like a caterpillar, from the heel to the toes. Repeat until you have thumb-crawled to each toe.

4. Massage toes. Grab the big toe with three fingers and rock it gently. Do the same motion with every toe.

All steps can be repeated 5-6 times on each foot.

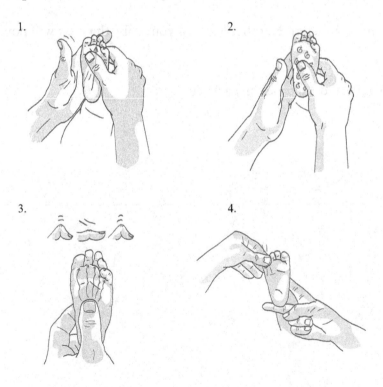

Chest

Warm up the oil between your palms. Keep both palms on your baby's chest for about 5–10 seconds and feel her heartbeat. Send warmth from your heart via your hands to your baby's chest. Say some comforting words with your soft voice.

1. The Heart. Rest your hands on the middle of the chest for a few seconds. Calmly, and in a grounded manner, sweep up towards the shoulders. Gliding down the side of the body, collect your hands below the navel and stroke up to the starting point.

2. The Open Book. Rest your hands in the middle of your baby's chest for a few seconds before you sweep your hands out to the side, as if opening a book.

3. The X. Rest both hands on her chest for a few seconds before you sweep the right hand up to the left shoulder and back. Do the same with your left hand: sweep it up to the right shoulder and back to the starting point. Once you have gained more experience with this exercise, you can gently squeeze around the shoulder joint.

All steps can be repeated 5-6 times.

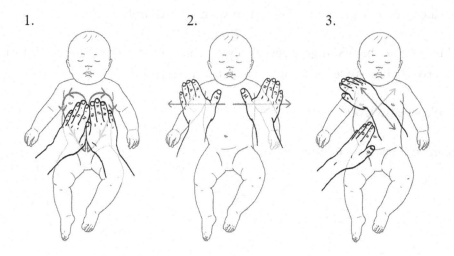

Arms

Heat the oil between the palms of your hands and distribute on your baby's one arm.

1. The C-grip. Form your hand like a C. Hold around the baby's arm at the armpit and sweep in a relaxed and gentle manner down over the elbow, forearm, hand and fingers. Alternate your hands.

2. Squeeze and slide. Place both hands on your baby's upper arm. Press lightly on the arm muscles until you feel resistance in the muscle, release, and without losing skin contact, slide calmly down to the forearm. Press lightly on the forearm and slide down to the fingers.

   Perform the same routine on the other arm. Tell your baby that you will now continue with the other arm.

All steps can be repeated 5-6 times on each arm.

Hands

1. Create circles inside your baby's palm with your thumb.

2. Massage your baby's fingers between your thumb and index finger. *«All are my favorite fingers»* is a fun nursery rhyme to use while massaging.

3. Stroke the back of the hand.

All steps can be repeated 5-6 times on each hand.

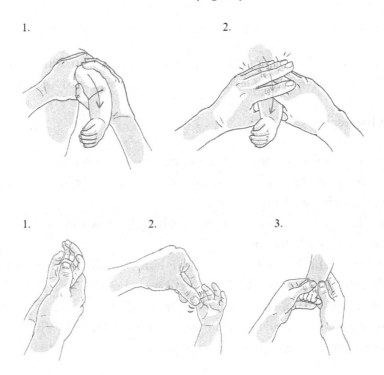

All are my favorite fingers

First little finger is called as thumb,
Second little finger is called as index,
Third little finger is called as middle,
Fourth little finger is called as ring,
And fifth little finger is called as little,
All are my favorite fingers,
And be with me as good friends ligers.

Week 2: Movement

Now that you are well underway with the massage, and your baby finds it exciting and fun and is ready for new challenges, you can try some fun, stimulating exercises that are developmental, and strengthening. Continue the basic massage strokes you have already learned for the next few weeks in addition to the new things you learn for this week.

Superstar

This exercise has two levels: One level for the smaller babies who don't have the strength to lift their heads by themselves, and a level for babies who are able to lift their heads.

For the smaller babies:

1. Lie down on your back with your knees bent and your feet on the ground.
2. Place the baby on your shins, so that the baby's chin rests between your knees. Keep eye contact with your baby.
3. Lift your legs up to a 90-degree angle. The baby lies flat and level to the ground. Hold firmly around your baby's body.
4. Raise your legs a little higher, so the baby is lying with his head slightly down and feels gravity pulling in the opposite direction of what he is used to.
5. Lower your legs again, so the baby restores a normal sense of gravity. You can do this exercise of raising and lowering your legs several times. When the baby becomes restless or indicates that he has had enough, stop.

Superstars who are in control of their head movements:

1. Lie down on your back with your knees bent and your feet on the ground.
2. Place the baby on your shins. Keep eye contact through the exercise, and throughout the exercise assess whether your baby can handle the challenges. Hold firmly around your baby's body.
3. Lift your legs up to a 90-degree angle. The baby lies flat and level to the ground.
4. Raise one leg a little, so that the baby will be slightly tilted. This will automatically induce your baby to attempt to stabilize himself using muscles from the opposite arm and leg, and this helps strengthen his back muscles.
5. Raise both your legs a little higher, so the baby is lying with his head slightly down and feels gravity pulling in the opposite direction of what he is used to.
6. Take a good grip around the baby's chest, lift him up, and let him slide down your shins, ending in a sitting position on your stomach. In this position, you can have a nice conversation or sing a happy song.

Bicycling

Let the baby's ankles rest in your palms. Alternately bend each knee up towards the baby's belly, while you carefully stretch the other leg, as if you are bicycling. Do the movements at a calm pace. Repeat 4–5 times.

Power pose stretch

Let your baby grasp your thumbs and stretch the arms out to each side. Cross the arms over the chest and stretch the arms out to each side again.

> Use enough oil, adding to your hands for each body part.

Week 3: Play and sensory stimulation

In addition to massage and movement we will focus on stimulating your baby with sounds and playful activities.

This playful song has fun coordination challenges.

"If you're happy and you know it…"

1st verse:
If you're happy and you know it, clap your hands
If you're happy and you know it, clap your hands
If you're happy and you know it, and you really want to show it
If you're happy and you know it clap your hands

The next few verses use the same lyrics but change the activity:

- bend your knees
- clap your knees
- close your eyes
- cross your arms and legs
- dance

- laugh
- put your hands on your stomach, shoulders, knees, hips
- reach for the sky
- shake your head, left leg, hand, right hand, leg
- touch your nose, mouth, toes
- wave goodbye

Be creative and move your and your baby's body to the lyrics, have fun together!

"Itsy-Bitsy Spider"

"The Itsy-Bitsy Spider, climbed up the water spout": Softly dance your fingers from the belly and up to the head, and shape your hands like a spout on the baby's head.

"Down came the rain and washed the spider out": Dance your fingertips down from the head to the belly, and keep your hands on your baby's belly and push gently while saying "out."

"Out came the sun and dried up all the rain": Hold your baby's hands and make a large circle with her arms, and raise her hands up to the head, touching the imaginary spout.

"And the itsy-bitsy spider climbed up the spout again": Dance your fingers all over the body, moving them upwards, ending on top of the head.

Week 4: Coordination

Now your baby is used to being touched, have moved around, played and been sung for. We can now start putting it all together with coordination exercises.

1. Cross arms over chest.
2. Cycle, alternating each leg
3. Clap your knees. Alternate hand to knee.
4. Touch your heart. Alternate with other hand.

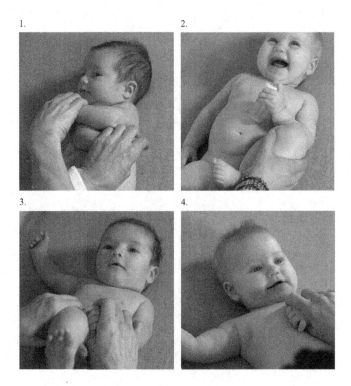

5. Dancing making hip circles.
6. Rock'n Roll.

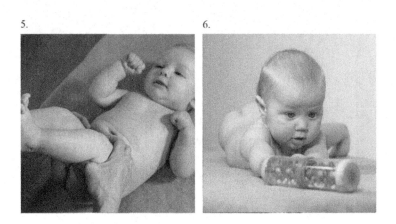

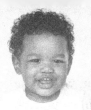

4

PLAYFUL COORDINATION AND BALANCE EXERCISES

Imagine that your child is born with wings. — Carolyn Parkhurst

Play is an important part of your baby's daily activities. From early on, the baby is ready for play and interaction with you and your family, her best playmates. Play is not done just for fun, it also helps the baby to understand the world and people around her, while she also develops an understanding of herself and her body. At the beginning of life, play means simply listening to the voices and the songs you sing or being cradled in your arms or lying on your lap looking at you. This interaction brings you closer and, combined with strokes and exercises, helps build communication and trust. It also strengthens physical coordination, body awareness, emotional security, and self-esteem. Incorporating play into your everyday activities gives your baby the greatest opportunity to develop her creativity and imagination.

Children laugh often when they are playing. Laughter reduces stress and strengthens the immune system. It is contagious!

It is fun to play with children. The greatest reward is to hear their joyful laughter! Find your inner child and become a playful dad or mom, then you will easily get to know what your child likes, what capabilities she has, and her personality. You will also discover new aspects of yourself. Recent research suggests that play, laughter, and conversation promote development at all levels: physically, mentally, emotionally, and socially.

Give your baby the opportunity to express herself during the day. It is important to use variation, so that she is stimulated and can develop. When massaging, you should vary between having your baby on her tummy and her back. When the child is carried, you should vary between the right and left sides. In this way, you help stimulate the neural pathways between the muscles and the brain, and this balances your baby's development of balance, strength, and coordination between the right and left sides of the body. This is especially important for your child in order to learn to crawl, which presupposes a certain muscle strength, balance, and understanding of the body to master the symmetrical gait, where the arms and legs are alternately swung forward and backward. It is the same movement pattern when the baby moves forward on the floor, an important precursor to first being able to crawl, and then walk. Let your baby lie on a soft surface, like a paraben-free exercise or yoga mat, so that she is not at risk of sliding and gains control of her movements.

Remember to have fun while you play together! Shared joy is double joy.

Fun coordination exercises

Head, shoulders, knees, and toes

Head, shoulders, knees, and toes is a great song, as it involves the whole body, is simple, can be done anywhere, and is suitable for all age groups. The song is also very easy to learn, and the baby gets a whole-body perspective, while her senses of rhythm, hearing, and attention are stimulated.

0-7 months, before your baby is able to sit:
Do the exercise while your baby is lying down on your lap, mat, or blanket.

When your baby can sit:
You may perform the exercise seated or lying down.

When your baby can stand:
You may perform the exercise standing, seated, or lying down.

When your child can walk:
Let her copy you and then "teach" you the body parts as you are singing.

Head, shoulders, knees and toes
Head, shoulders, knees, and toes, knees and toes
Head, shoulders, knees and toes, knees and toes
Eyes and ears and mouth and nose to touch
Head, shoulders, knees, and toes, knees and toes!

Superstar

This is a great exercise and a fun activity that develops the interaction between you and your baby, while the baby also gets an understanding of herself and the world around her – using gravity, for instance. This exercise has two levels: One level for the smaller babies who don't have the strength to lift their heads by themselves, and a level for babies who are able to lift their heads.

For the smaller babies:

1. Lie down on your back with your knees bent and your feet on the ground.
2. Place the baby on your shins, so that the baby's chin rests between your knees. Keep eye contact with your baby.
3. Lift your legs up to a 90-degree angle. The baby lies flat and level to the ground. Hold firmly around your baby's body.
4. Raise your legs a little higher, so the baby is lying with his head slightly down and feels gravity pulling in the opposite direction of what he is used to.
5. Lower your legs again, so the baby restores a normal sense of gravity. You can do this exercise of raising and lowering your legs several times. When the baby becomes restless or indicates that he has had enough, stop.

Superstars who are in control of their head movements:

1. Lie down on your back with your knees bent and your feet on the ground.
2. Place the baby on your shins. Keep eye contact through the exercise, and throughout the exercise assess whether your baby can handle the challenges. Hold firmly around your baby's body.
3. Lift your legs up to a 90-degree angle. The baby lies flat and level to the ground.
4. Raise one leg a little, so that the baby will be slightly tilted. This will automatically induce your baby to attempt to stabilize himself using muscles from the opposite arm and leg, and this helps strengthen his back muscles.
5. Raise both your legs a little higher, so the baby is lying with his head slightly down and feels gravity pulling in the opposite direction of what he is used to.
6. Take a good grip around the baby's chest, lift him up, and let him slide down your shins, ending in a sitting position on your stomach. In this position, you can have a nice conversation or sing a happy song.

Be aware of your baby's need for breaks.

Trampoline (1–6 months)

Let your baby sit on your lap. Hold around her waist. Lift her up in the air and let her feet just barely touch your lap before lifting again. You can sing a song or a nursery rhyme.

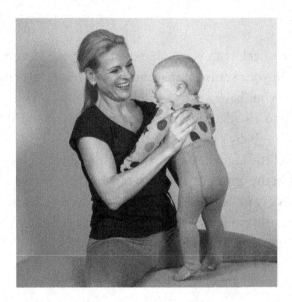

The trampoline is a great exercise for you as well, strengthening your arm and shoulder muscles! If you twist a little while lifting your baby from side to side, it's a perfect strengthening and toning exercise for your waist! Triple joy!!

Rolling (2–6 months)

When your baby is lying on her back or tummy, you can inspire her to roll around by holding a toy in front of or behind her so that she must stretch to reach the toy. Support the baby's bottom with your hand, making it easier to turn to one side or the other until she can master the challenge by herself.

Age-appropriate exercises

0–3 months

- Baby mobile: The baby lies on his back and can stretch towards the toys that appear as bright colors in front of his face. This strengthens the neck and back, as well as stimulates the visual senses.
- The baby lies on his tummy with interesting toys in front of his face. Vary the toy's distance from 6 to 12 inches (15 to 30 cm), and vary the location of the toy from in front, to the right, and to the left of the baby.
- Songs/rhymes with appropriate touch and movements:
  - Head, shoulders, knees and toes
  - Itsy Bitsy Spider
  - When you're happy and you know it
  - Eeny, Meeny, Miny Moe
  - All the sharks in the sea

3–6 months

- **The Pilot Flying The Fantastic Fantasy Airplane**
  Sit or stand, hold around your baby's chest, and lift her up in the air. You can, for instance, say, "Are you ready for a flight? Now we're going to fly, 1, 2, 3." Then lift her

up. Say something about the flight, about the places you are flying to, and what you see. Turn the baby around and fly around the room, if possible.

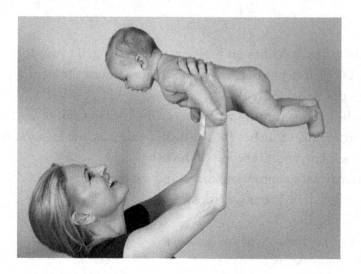

- **Rolling**
When your baby is lying on her back or tummy, you can inspire her to turn around by holding a toy in front of or behind her so that she must stretch. Support the baby's bottom with your hand so that it is easier for her to turn to one side or the other.

- **Pat-a Cake or The seasons**, on your lap.

Pat-a Cake
Pat-a Cake, Pat-a Cake, baker's man!
Bake me a cake as fast as you can;
Roll it and pat it and mark it with "B,"
And put it in the oven for baby and me

The seasons
Spring is showery, flowery, bowery;
Summer: hoppy, croppy, poppy
Autumn: wheezy, sneezy, freezy;
Winter: slippy, drippy, nippy

- **Baby mobile**
  The baby lies on her back and can stretch towards the toys that appear as bright colors in front of her face. This strengthens the neck, back, and develops the baby's senses.

- The baby lies on her tummy with interesting toys in front of her face. Vary the toy's distance from 6 to 12 inches (15 to 30 cm), and vary the location of the toy from in front, to the right, and to the left of the baby.

6–9 months

- **Trampoline**
  The baby is sitting on your lap. Hold around the baby's waist and lift her up in the air, and let her feet only barely touch your lap before lifting again. You can sing a song or a nursery rhyme.

- **Song**
  "The sharks in the sea", see page 69.

The baby lies on her back and you move her arm and opposite ankle toward each other, alternating legs and arms. The first verse of the song *The Sharks in the sea* is perfect for this exercise. Be creative and do appropriate movements for the other verses of the song.

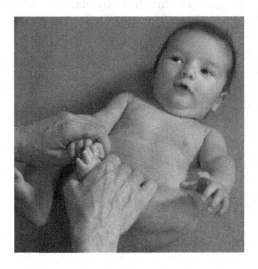

- **Mirror**
Let your baby look at herself in the mirror to be familiar with her face.

- **Rattle in hand**

  It makes a sound when the baby is moving. Great discovery!

- **Crawling over you**
Suddenly you become a climbing frame and a fun, inspiring play partner.

9–12 months

- **How big is baby?**
Sit with your baby on the floor, on your lap on the couch, or in a chair. "How big is baby? Sooooooo big." And lift the baby's arms above her head. Eventually, your baby will lift her arms above her head when you ask how big she is.

- **Variant of the trampoline**
Mom or dad sits with one leg crossed over the other and places the baby on the ankle. Hold your baby by the hands, and gently rock the leg up and down.

- **Walking challenge**
Challenge your walking or crawling baby by placing some obstacles on the floor, such as a sofa cushion, and let the baby have a reward, like a building block or a rattle, at the other end.

- **Ball game**
The baby sits on the floor and you roll a ball toward her.

- **Tower**
Build a tower by stacking building blocks. Tearing down the tower is even more fun.

- Cover toys with blanket and let her find her toys.

- Play music and dance.

- Playing in the bathtub with foam and different toys.

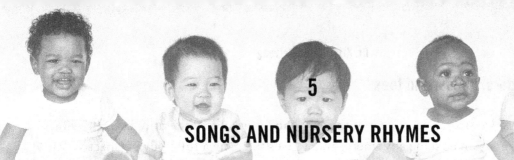

5

SONGS AND NURSERY RHYMES

Our time together can be made into a fun, stimulating, and wonderful time by singing a song, counting 1, 2, 3..., or using a nursery rhyme while massaging. This sets the pace for the movements while it also puts your baby in an expectant mood and also develops his sense of rhythm, balance, coordination and helps connect words to the different body parts. The baby likes communicating through melody and loves your voice and the way you talk. Your voice is familiar and safe from the time he was in your womb. From week 24 onward during pregnancy, the sense of hearing starts to develop. The fetus can distinguish between different voices in the environment and the difference between male and female voices (mom and dad). Singing has a stress-reducing effect on babies and is commonly used at bedtime to calm the baby down and induce sleep. It prefers your familiar voice rather than the radio.

Researchers believe that well-known children's songs and traditional nursery rhymes are strong tools that help prepare children's brains to learn language – so parents should sing to their children every day. They also believe that this will prevent language problems later in life. Singing is a particular type of speech, and nursery rhymes in every culture have their own "signature" that primes the child's ear, voice, and brain for language. Also, the child learns a text faster when it is sung.

Wake your inner child and sing with the voice you have. Song communicates respect. Connect generations singing the same song that were song for you. Explore through play, smiles, laughter, and positivity – it is contagious!

When you sing, use the baby's name: Baby loves to hear her name.

Head, shoulders, knees, and toes

Head, shoulders, knees, and toes is a favorite song – and it involves the entire body. It's simple, easy to learn, and can be done anywhere, and it gives the baby a full-body perspective while also stimulating a sense of rhythm, hearing, and attention. While you sing, lightly touch the appropriate body part accordingly. You may also guide his hands to each body part and let him touch her head, shoulders, eyes, ears, nose, chin, mouth, knees, and toes.

Text:
Head, shoulders, knees, and toes, knees and toes
Head, shoulders, knees and toes, knees and toes
Eyes and ears and mouth and nose to touch
Head, shoulders, knees, and toes, knees and toes!

This little piggy

This nursey rhyme is used when playing, touching, and massaging the toes, the small and sweet tiny baby «piggies». Start with the big toe on one foot, and go through each toe, rocking each between your fingers on each foot while telling the story about the little piggies going to market. Vary the tone of your voice and make it a fun little game. Your baby thinks it is great fun to learn the rhyme and hear the anticipation in your voice. Eventually he will participate himself and extend his foot to you. It's a fun interaction and strengthens the bond between you.

Text:
This little piggy went to market
This little piggy stayed home
This little piggy had roast beef
And this little piggy had none
This little piggy went "wee wee wee wee wee,"
all the way home!

Shoe my pony

This is a nice rhyme to hum while massaging the soles and toes of the baby. It is based on a Norwegian nursery rhyme. In the first sentence, you should stroke your baby's foot, and in the second sentence massage each toe.

Text:
Shoe my pony, shoe my horse
Which little toooe is on the right course?
1: Is it THIS one?
2: Or THIS toe?
3: Maybe it is THE one?
4: Could it be This?
5: Yes! THIS is the one!

Have enthusiasm in your voice and use positive words.

All are my favorite fingers

This is a delightful finger rhyme that makes your baby familiar with the hands and fingers.

Text:
First little finger is called as thumb,
Second little finger is called as index,
Third little finger is called as middle,
Fourth little finger is called as ring,
And fifth little finger is called as little,
All are my favorite fingers,
And be with me as good friends ligers.

Itsy-bitsy spider

This nursey rhyme strengthens your interaction with your baby and your baby's body awareness – and will make you both laugh, for sure!

Text:
The Itsy-bitsy spider, climbed up the water spout
Down came the rain and washed the spider out
Out came the sun and dried up all the rain
And the itsy-bitsy spider climbed up the spout again

People who sing tend to be happy.

Eeny, meeny, miny, moe

Alternate between touching the baby and yourself during this nursery rhyme.

Text:
Eeny, meeny, miny, moe
Catch a tiger by the toe
If he hollers let him go!
Eeny, meeny, miny, moe.

Or:
Eeny, meeny, miny, moe
Catch a <u>piggy</u> by the toe
If he hollers let him go!
Eeny, meeny, miny, moe.

Or:
Eeny, meeny, miny, moe
Catch a <u>monkey</u> by the toe
If he hollers let him go!
Eeny, meeny, miny, moe.

Please feel free to change the animal to something else – maybe you have a favorite animal, a pet, a friend, or a neighbor you would like to include!

> Be a flexible and cheerful parent. You
> are an inspiration to your baby.

Row, row, row your boat

Here you row with your baby's hands and point at siblings and relevant family members according to the lyrics.

Text:
Row, row, row your boat
Gently down the stream
Merrily, merrily, merrily, merrily
Life is but a dream!

Row, row, row your boat
Gently up the creek If you see a little mouse
Don't forget to squeak!

Row, row, row your boat
Gently down the stream If you see a crocodile
Don't forget to scream!

Row, row, row your boat
Gently to the shore
If you see a lion
Don't forget to roar!

Humpty Dumpty

The baby sits slightly higher than you, for example, on a table. Holding your baby tight, make and keep eye contact, and as you sing, let your baby slide down a little when you get to the appropriate point in the song. The surprise in the "fall" and the anticipation and surprise in the tone of your voice, will daze and amaze the little one, who will laugh enthusiastically every time! It's fun for the whole family.

Text:
Humpty Dumpty sat on a wall.
Humpty Dumpty had a great fall.
All the king's horses and all the king's men
couldn't put Humpty together again.

Pat-a Cake

This delicious rhyme is perfect to do when, for instance, you are changing diapers, tapping on your baby's chest and tummy. Follow the text, be creative, and have fun with this rhyme!

Text:
Pat-a Cake, Pat-a Cake, baker's man!
Bake me a cake as fast as you can;
Roll it and pat it and mark it with "B,"
And put it in the oven for baby and me.

The seasons

Text:
Spring is showery, flowery, bowery;
Summer: hoppy, croppy, poppy
Autumn: wheezy, sneezy, freezy;
Winter: slippy, drippy, nippy

Days of the week

Text:
Monday alone,
Tuesday together
Wednesday we walk, in the weather

Thursday, we kiss
Friday, we cry
Saturday's hours seem almost to fly.
But of all the days of the week we will call
Sundays, the rest day,
The best day of all.

Bow-Wow, says the Dog

Text:
Bow-wow, says the dog;
Mew, mew, says the cat;
Grunt, grunt, goes the hog;
And squeak says the rat.
Tu-whu, says the owl;
Caw-caw, goes the crow;
Quack-quack, goes the duck;
And moo, says the cow.

If you're happy and you know it…

Text:
1st verse:
If you're happy and you know it, clap your hands
If you're happy and you know it, clap your hands
If you're happy and you know it, and you really want to show it
If you're happy and you know it clap your hands

The next few verses use the same lyrics but change the activity:

- bend your knees
- clap your knees
- close your eyes
- cross your arms and legs
- dance

- laugh
- put your hands on your stomach, shoulders, knees, hips
- reach for the sky
- shake your head, left leg, hand, right hand, leg
- touch your nose, mouth, toes
- wave goodbye
- wave with your hands

Be creativeand move your and your baby's body to the lyrics, have fun together!

The sharks in the sea

Tune: The wheels on the bus

Text:
The sharks in the sea goes chomp, chomp, chomp.
chomp, chomp, chomp
chomp, chomp, chomp
The sharks in the sea goes chomp, chomp, chomp.
All day long!

The lobster in the sea go pinch...
The fish in the sea goes swim...
The clams in the sea goes open and shut...
The octopus in the sea goes wiggle...
The seahorse in the sea rocks back and forth...
The kids in the waves jump up and down...

Babies and kids love to move their body to the lyrics.
Have fun and sing together!

6
UNCOMPLICATED EVERYDAY AILMENTS

There are several strokes and exercises you can perform on your baby which will provide relief for various kinds of everyday ailments.

Colic/stomachache

Colic is a condition where a healthy baby cries inconsolably, often during the afternoon and evening over a longer stretch of time, up to three to five months of age. 10–15 percent of all children get colic. The symptoms usually come during the first two to four weeks after birth. There are many theories about what colic really is, but in general it is viewed as an overall irritation of the digestive system. Colic is not dangerous.

Signs of colic:

- intermittent, unexplained, intense screaming in an otherwise healthy child
- legs often retracted towards the tummy
- head and torso bent backwards when the child cries
- restless leg and arm movements, fisted hands
- baby is often inconsolable
- baby is awake a lot and sleeps only for shorter periods of time

One technique that can be soothing for babies with gastrointestinal problems: The baby lies on her stomach supported on your arms.

Map your child's crying pattern and perform tummy regulatory exercises around ½ hour before crying. See page 73 for instructions.

It is important that you give your child the opportunity to burp in order to expel air. Please be patient.

Burping Technique 1

You are seated. Place your baby's legs between your legs so that you have control of the baby, and place one hand on the upper part of the abdomen while the fingers support the jaw. The other hand is placed on the upper back and back of the head and neck.

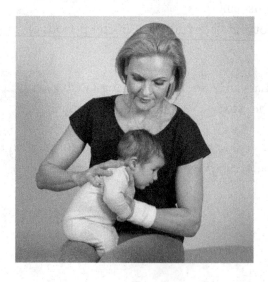

Burping Technique 2

Rest the child's upper body on your shoulder (supporting the baby's head if she does not have head control) and stroke one hand up along the back from the baby's bottom.

.

Stomach-regulating exercises

To relieve colic symptoms, there are some massage techniques that help babies who are uncomfortable. Perform all exercises daily in the outlined order, two to three times successively, ½ hour before the crying usually starts. Use a soft teddy bear, a pacifier, or anything that can comfort and divert attention during the massage. Never force the baby into a position she doesn't want to be in. You can invite her to participate by telling her what will happen next. The exercises are good to use regardless of all ailments, and are also used on babies who are without symptoms and don't have a stomach ache. Exercise performed before or around ½ hour after the meal.

1. The Waterfall. Stroke your palms with medium pressure on the tummy right below the rib cage down towards the hip. Six repetitions.

2. Keep the knees together and bend them towards the baby's tummy, without moving the hip. Keep position for around six seconds. Calmly extend the legs.

3. Circle and arc. Make a circle on the baby's belly with one palm, and an arc with the other. Follow a clockwise direction. Do the circle and arc simultaneously. Six repetitions.

4. Repeat: keep the knees together and bend towards the belly, without moving the hip. Hold for about six seconds. Calmly extend the legs.

5. The Screw. Hold around the baby's thighs and, with gathered knees, rotate the legs in a clockwise direction, to just above the navel, in a small movement, about six circles. Calmly extend the legs.

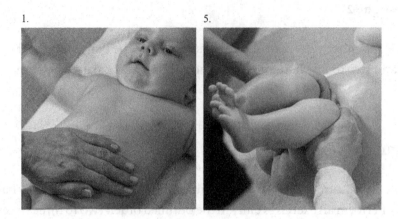

The routine should preferably be performed three times daily. It's easy to do when changing diapers and during washing and general care. It may take several days before you see positive results if your aim is to alleviate intestinal problems and pain.

Stomach pain – a personal story

One Thursday, the parents of eight-week-old Sofia entered my office. They were exhausted and desperate. Sofia wept inconsolably. The last five to six weeks they had carried her from midday to midnight, trying everything to calm her, without success. Both mom and dad took turns carrying, lulling, taking her in the baby stroller, driving the car, and vacuuming around Sofia to calm her. The grandparents gave a helping hand so the parents could get some sleep and recover after weeks of exhaustion. Their neighbor could hear Sofia and suggested that they see me, a chiropractor.

It was clear that they were all tired. Both mom and dad came to the consultation. Together they could provide a complete picture of the pregnancy, birth, the time at home after birth, and Sofia's symptoms.

The mom had been nauseous during the pregnancy, but mostly felt healthy and fit and worked until the end of the prescribed time. There were a lot of fetal movements throughout her pregnancy, and a control at the clinic and at their GP's office showed normal growth and development. All blood samples and other samples were normal. When the contractions started, they went to the hospital, the birth had started. Sofia came quickly. Everything was normal and they went home after a few days. Sofia gained weight and slept normally. She had some irregular bowel movements and swallowed some air while breastfeeding.

Two to three weeks after she was born, the wailing began. Eventually they recognized a pattern. At 6 p.m. Sofia started crying violently, retracted her legs to her tummy, flailed her arms, and clenched her fists. The stomach was tense and «bulging», they explained. Whatever they did, they could not comfort her or calm her down.

These are typical signs of colic pain or gastrointestinal intestinal problems. But other conditions may still be present. Upon examination, I could assess that Sofie was developing normally. Reflexes were normal for her stage of development, she had symmetrical movements of arms and legs and otherwise no limitations of the musculoskeletal system. But her tummy was tight and felt tense and full. Sofia was treated with a light manual adjustment. Furthermore, the parents were trained to perform the massage exercises to alleviate stomach pain and techniques for releasing air, as well as other soothing techniques. Sofia was completely at ease during the treatment. We set up a new appointment the week after.

The situation had improved somewhat when we met for the next appointment. Mom and dad alternated doing the exercises and were in good spirits. We continued with treatment and home exercises, and a few weeks later the condition had improved significantly: she seemed happy and slept better and longer, both during the day and night, and all in all seemed to be a whole lot happier.

The parents felt that they had done something positive for Sofia, and it felt good. They felt empowered in their parenting through helping her get better. They also felt closer to each other, as they had a common task they could collaborate on that would improve Sofia's daily life. I have seen Sofia retrospectively – she is a harmonious baby without any ailments. The parents still have to massage her belly, and they have participated in my courses and learned the whole massage program, which they all have enjoyed.

Note to parents: Chiropractors are health care professionals who specializes in the diagnoses and treatment of neuromuscular disorders. They have special training in manual adjustments, techniques, which they use to adjust the spine and eliminate the cause of health problems. If the baby's joints are being treated, the pressure applied to the respective joints is approximately the same pressure you can tolerate on a closed eye. The treatment will relax and soothe most infants. Giving advice to parents is an essential part of the treatment. Advice about massage and touch, breastfeeding and bottle feeding, sleep routines, and carrying techniques are some of the topics that are dealt with.

Cradle Cap

Cradle Cap causes crusty or oily scaly patches on a baby's scalp and is also known as seborrheic dermatitis. It's a common and benign condition the first 3 to 4 months after birth but may also appear later. It is caused by the buildup of oil and the shedding of skin cells. Redness, yellow or white greasy scales, and heavy flaking appears on the scalp.

It is not harmful to your baby.

You can treat cradle cap yourself by applying and massage the organic homemade oil to the scales on the scalp, daily until it is gone. Soft brushing can also help remove the scales. (If this doesn't work, consult your pediatrician. She may prescribe a stronger shampoo or an ointment.)

Baby Acne

Are small pimples that looks similar to adult acne, breaking out on the face, typically during the fourth or fifth week of life, and are harmless. Doctors believe the acne is caused by pregnancy hormones stimulating the oil glands in the skin of the baby. Please do not try to pop the blemish but gently wash your baby's face with lukewarm water once a day. Avoid laundering the crib sheets in harsh and perfumed detergents.

Colds and light respiratory ailments

To ease tension and pain, ache, discomfort and irritations, use these strokes on your baby's chest. Refer to page 25 for exercise 1-4. Do all or select 2.

1. The Heartbeat.
2. The Heart.
3. The Open book.
4. The X.

5. Clavicle: The clavicle is located directly below the throat on the upper part of the chest. Swipe below the clavicle with your fingertips, from the breastbone and towards the shoulder joints. For greater impact, shape your fingers into Cs or Os.

6. Throat: With your palms, stroke upwards on the throat. You can use essential oil of eucalyptus, which you make by mixing a finger drop (what you get on your finger when you turn the bottle upside down) with the oil in your hand. It opens the airways and makes it a little easier to breathe. Remember to wash the mixture off your hands before massaging elsewhere.

7. Face: Hold two fingers on each side of the lower part of the nose for about three seconds and let go. Repeat three times. Do the same between the eyebrows. You need not use extra oil in the face; just touch the skin lightly with what is already on your hands.

8. Massage around the eye socket: Go along the eyebrows to the temple and make circles three times on the temple and continue under the eye, along the eye socket from the nose to the temple.

9. Ear: Massage the ear cartilage and lobe between your fingers. Here you can have a close interaction since your faces are close together. Take the opportunity to sing or hum a nursery rhyme or, for instance, say something about the present day. Maybe you could say something about the positive effects the baby will get from what you are doing.

Umbilical cord

A newborn's umbilical cord stump typically dries out and falls off within two weeks after birth. In the meantime, treat your baby's umbilical cord stump gently.

After bathing pat dry the area around the navel. Keep the area dry and fold down the diaper so it will not rub against the healing umbilical cord. Resist the temptation of pulling it out, let it heal completely and fall off by itself, avoiding a possible infection and a longer wound healing time.

Umbilical Granuloma

After the umbilical cord stump have dried up and fallen off, within a few weeks of birth, very seldom the base of the cord forms a growth called a granuloma. The area around the umbilical cord may be moist and swell slightly, turn yellow and could ooze or bleed a little bit. It is not painful and looks worse than it is.

Your pediatrician might treat this using silver nitrate to dry it out. If that doesn't work, it may have to be removed in a minor procedure.

Umbilical Hernia

An umbilical Hernia is a bulge that you can see or feel at the belly button area caused by a small gap in the abdominal wall that allows tissue to bulge out when there's pressure inside the abdomen (for example when a baby cries or strains). It is clearly visible when your baby seems to push outward when she cries.

Most umbilical hernias heal themselves in the first 12 to 18 months. If your child's hernia doesn't heal by the time he enters school, your pediatrician may suggest minor surgery.

Fever

The body temperature will rise from normal temperature, at approximately 97,2 -99,5 F (36,2 – 37,5 degrees Celsius), when the body is invaded by a virus or a bacteria as a natural immune response. The immune system operates efficiently at 100.4–102.2 F (38–39 degrees C), defeating infections. In these circumstances, the baby has a fever. You can measure the temperature in the baby's bottom (rectally) a few times a day to monitor developments. If there is a minor infection, the temperature should drop within a few days or at most within a week, but if the temperature remains elevated, at 102.2–104 F (39 to 40 degrees C) or above, and the baby's general condition is reduced, you should consult a health care professional. Infants less than three months old with a fever should be examined by a doctor.

Symptoms of fever:

- Baby is lethargic, distant, fearful
- Reduced appetite and thirst, resulting in a dry diaper (dehydration)
- Cold hands and feet
- Pale and gray skin around the mouth

Babies less than one year old should only get fever-reducing medication in consultation with a doctor.

The skin becomes extra sensitive with increased body temperature, so it is not favorable to perform infant massage or interact playfully. Instead, make sure that the baby can rest as much as possible and offer lots of fluids to avoid dehydration. Add a damp cloth to the baby's head which will feel soothing.

Teeth (teething)

When the teeth break through the gums, the surrounding area may get a little irritated. You can recognize the symptoms, as the baby will put everything she can find in her mouth and drool more than usual.

Action: Gently massage the baby's gums, with clean fingers. Press gently against the gum and let your baby push the gums together against your finger as if chewing on your finger to releave itching. You can also try using a paraben-free teething ring that has been in the refrigerator. The coolness of the teething ring soothes pain and itching in the gums, while the resistance makes it easier for the teeth to break through.

Sleep

Some babies sleep more than others, and others sleep less than average. There are individual differences here, as in everything else in life. Parents should not compare their babies with other babies in this area, either. The average daily need for sleep is:

1 month: 16.5 h
3 months: 15 h
6 months: 14.5 h
1 year: 13.75 h

The hours indicated, include periods of sleep during the day and at night.

Night sleep is important for many stages of development, and to establish the circadian rhythms that are regulated by the biological clock. It is thus greatly beneficial for the baby to find this rhythm. By having regular routines, the baby will be able to find her own biological clock. Babies thrive on routine and predictability, and it's okay to have regular routines as early as six weeks of age. Research shows that introducing four fixed elements each evening may regulate a baby's biological clock. By using baby massage as one of these four routines at bedtime, you can get a good ending to the day and, also very important, a good start to the night.

Babies should "find sleep" by themselves, in the same way when adults go to bed, settle down and sleep. It is normal that she wakes up during the night. If your baby is safe and used to going to sleep by herself, she'll just turn around and go back to sleep. If a baby is used to being lulled, pushed in a stroller, or rocked to sleep, she will naturally seek the stimuli that causes her to sleep again, both upon awakening during the day and at night.

Researchers believe that these four routines have a great effect on sleep and that a large percentage of babies get longer and deeper sleep if you do the following:

1. Decide on a time, for example, somewhere between 6:30 p.m. - 7:30 p.m. Begin preparations for putting your baby to bed.
2. Choose one grooming routine that's right for your family, for example, body wash or a bath.
3. Massage the baby. The "good night" routine can fit nicely. See page 40.
4. Put the baby in bed, sing a song, talk about what you experienced during the day. Tell the baby that "Good night my love, it's nighttime and you can sleep safely until tomorrow." If she wakes up, say the same thing again.

By doing this every night, it becomes a pattern and a routine for the baby. Gradually she understands what is expected when the night comes. But if the routine is disrupted by illness or travel, the routine will have to be resumed when you return, or when the baby is healthy again.

Other studies show that through regular massage, more of the hormone melatonin is secreted. Melatonin is known as the sleep hormone.

Problems with sleep

If your baby is restless and can't sleep, these simple strokes, your quiet, safe touch and calm voice will be relaxing. All the following strokes can be done with clothes on. Notice which strokes seems to be most relaxing. Some babies prefer less touch and prefer a gentle song or a lullaby. All strokes can be done as long as it is comfortable for the baby. Try all the exercises a few times and explore what works best for you.

In bed:

1. Stroke with your palm gently and lightly over her forehead and nose. Multiple times.
2. Stroke with your palm gently and lightly down along the body.
3. Stroke with your palm gently and lightly under and on the inside of the sole of the foot.
4. Stroke with your palm gently and lightly from the calf and down to the toes.

Blocked Tear Ducts

You will observe water tearing and/or sticky mucus in the corner of the eye.

It is a harmless condition were tear ducts are blocked and occurs when the baby is born with one or both of the tear ducts partially or fully blocked.

Tear ducts usually open by the time a baby is 2 weeks old.

The ducts will usually open without treatment, but you may gently massage the inner corner of the eye to help them open.

Environmental pollution

It is important to be aware that environmental toxins are everywhere. The skin is our largest organ, and everything is absorbed through it. Environmental toxins interfere with the hormonal balance in the body and negatively affect fertility, allergies, and asthma. It is therefore important to take good care of the small developing bodies and protect them in the best possible way.

> Always wash new clothes before your baby uses them the first time. There are dyes and other chemicals in clothing. These substances may enter the baby's body, and the body must work hard to get rid of them.

Reduce the use of wipes with fragrance. Chemicals from wet wipes in a delicate area should be used with caution and preferably not at all. Buy either cloth or paper towels which can be wetted with water, when changing the baby's diapers or cleaning mouth or fingers.

7
PERSONAL STORIES

Twins participating in a «baby development» course

I was visiting a family who recently had twins. These were the couple's first children. They experienced family life with two babies as challenging and demanding, and they felt that the day was over before it had begun. The babies slept at different times, one was awake while the other slept. It was difficult getting into a daily routine as one activity happened before another had ended. The daily outing with the baby stroller was, however, a positive shared experience. During those outings, all four got a nice break.

I suggested that the parents could try baby massage with the twins. This, I thought, would establish a regular routine, as a common activity and enable the babies to sleep at the same time.

Since they wanted to focus on the bedtime routines I was with them the first evening and showed them some basic baby massage exercises they should do every night for the first week. Both parents and babies enjoyed themselves. The usual bedtime routine continued after the massage.

A week later, I returned. The parents told me that they looked forward to the new bedtime routines and that the babies fell asleep faster than before. They slept longer and were more coordinated than earlier.

Since this had worked so well, I asked if they would attend a course in baby massage. All four of them joined the course, as the baby massage had such a positive effect on the twins. In the baby massage room, there were six other babies with parents. The room was full of excitement. There were sounds from the others and interesting things to watch for the babies, which kept them awake.

The parents told me that after each course session, both babies fell asleep on the way home and thus they got more common sleeping time. This in turn made the parents enjoy doing baby massage together as frequently as they could. The parents thought that the course was a very good break from the daily hustle and bustle with the babies, and they appreciated that they could share these moments together as a family.

Now the babies are three years old, and all four are still enjoying massage almost every night.

Premature baby

Ellen gave birth to a little boy, Noah, in week 30 of her pregnancy. There were complications during the pregnancy, so the decision was made to deliver him early. The scheduled caesarean section was carried out without any problems. Noah was of normal size for his age, although he was small compared to babies born after a full-term pregnancy. Because he was born prematurely, his lungs were underdeveloped and he had to lie in an incubator for a while. This was hard to bear for his mother. She wanted so much to have Noah physically close to her, and the fact that he was lying in an incubator made her doubt whether they would develop the important bond that she wanted and had envisioned.

At the hospital, she got great follow-up from both the doctors and nurses, and she was taught kangaroo care. This is a method that is used for premature babies, with one of the parents reclining in a comfortable chair with the baby on their chest – skin-to-skin – large parts of the day and night. Studies show that premature are given kangaroo care, they do very well. They increase their uptake of nutrients, gain weight, improve their digestion and overall well-being, and get a well-regulated heart rate.

After Ellen was introduced to kangaroo care and spent many long and nurturing days with Noah on her chest, she felt very close to him. She felt she really got to know him.

She contacted me shortly after they came home from the hospital. She learned simple strokes she could perform on the tiny body. The skin of premature babies is very thin and lacks the underlying fat layer that children born full term have developed. They thus loose more heat and fluids, and lotions and oils that lubricate the skin are more easily absorbed into the body. The mom was aware of this, and she only used oil she had made herself from the best organic cold pressed extra virgin oils.

Noah continued to put on weight and grew at a normal pace. Gradually we introduced regular baby massage strokes, and they got into their own routines. Baby massage was an important part of their everyday life, for dad, mom, and Noah. Dad was inspired to learn more about how he could participate, and the dad routine quickly became their time together. The parents believe this has had a beneficial effect on Noah's positive development. It has been especially important for them to feel useful; like they help Noah in the somewhat rough beginning of life.

Restless and irritable baby who became calmer

A stressed mom and dad paced up and down the hallway in the waiting room, trying to lull and calm down six-week-old Sarah before they entered my consultation room. I felt for the young parents. After greeting all three of them and asking if I could hold Sarah, I took her in my arms. The parents sat down in the chairs and exhaled. They said nothing.

I walked around the office and tried to calm down Sarah, without any luck. I asked if it was okay to undress Sarah. They nodded. When I had taken off all her clothes (which I do to test reflexes and movement of joints in the arms and legs), loosened her diaper, and stroked her tiny body while speaking with a soothing voice, she paused and gave me a quizzical look.

Now mom came and sat down next to the examination table and told me about her pregnancy. It was a good pregnancy without complications until the eighth month. Then it was revealed she had high blood pressure and protein in her urine. She was sent to the hospital and examined carefully. It did not take many days before the condition got worse, and she was diagnosed with preeclampsia – little Sarah had to get out. The birth was initiated three weeks before the due date. Everything went as planned, and they went home after a short time.

It was a tough start for the little family as they had no previous experience with babies. Breastfeeding problems as was lack of sleep during the day and night for all three. Sarah were not able to rest, not in bed, stroller, car seat, nor in the arms of her parents. They were all frustrated. At a clinic, the medical doctor diagnosed her with symptoms of colic. This was also my conclusion, however I also thought she seemed very sensitive, to sounds and unexpected movements during dressing and undressing and being lifted and moved on the changing mat. In addition the parents told me that Sarah kicked her legs, pulled her legs towards her tummy, made fists, tensed into an arch, screamed, turned red, and was inconsolable usually in the evening.

With parental consent, I mobilized one part of her spine and massaged her stomach. I instructed the parents in many of the same massage techniques, and I facilitated a program for them that they could perform on Sarah every day. This became the dad's task, and he chose the evening time to do this, making it their time together. Mom was delighted that the two of them could share responsibility for the baby in this challenging phase, and that they had specific tasks: Dad took the evening care and bedtime routine, and mom's task was the feeding trough out the day. Eventually they developed a daily routine which was a lot easier for the small family.

Sarah had two more treatments over a three-week period. At the same time, the parents kept up their routines, including massage before bedtime. After a short time, they reported that they had a "brand new baby" who was satisfied throughout the day and night.

Often, it doesn't take much for a condition to improve. It doesn't have to be more than a precise, light push, with minimal force on a certain joint, and a massage of the surrounding muscles and connective tissues. With careful and thorough instruction, parents can perform the massage on their baby themselves.

Adopted baby

Adrian is a boy who was adopted when he was 19 months old. The first few months of his life he lived with parents who were busy with other things than being a parent. He got irregular meals, was not carried much, and only occasionally got care and cuddles. Because of the insufficient care, physical closeness was challenging for him.

Now massage and touch with positive intention is one of the activities that makes him feel safe. It has taken time for him to get used to this kind of contact. At first, he did not like to be touched, and he withdrew from all types of touch. The adoptive mom found alternative ways to touch him. She stroked him lightly across the back when she carried him, and she did the same when she washed him and dressed him. All care and touch were with positive intention. Slowly but surely, he became more responsive to touch, and now he prefers that it is combined with song and nursery rhymes. The adoptive mom consciously used songs and nursey rhymes as part of the efforts to improve Adrian's language development.

The adoptive parents set aside time each day to continue the routine and structure of these activities, and they see the joy Adrian gets from it and how useful it is for him. The aim in the long run is that he will be socialized and feel completely safe in all situations.

Adopted babies and parents can bond equally well as biological parents and their babies. The time it takes may vary. Please trust yourself and your own efforts. You are doing the best you can, and that is all you can do.

The time you spend playing, massaging and observing, gives you a deeper understanding of your baby's body and how it works.

8
PRESENCE – MINDFULNESS

Be happy in the moment, that's enough. Each moment is all we need, not more.

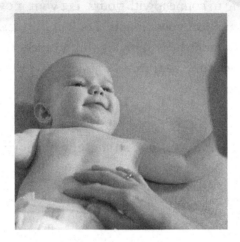

The key to mindfulness is the ability to be present in the moment – to be able to direct your thoughts and senses to what is happening around you in this moment. These are important elements to have in mind when you massage your baby with heartfelt intention. When you are fully present the interaction, playing and massage will feel deeper.

> Be fully present and enjoy every moment together.

Enjoy the feeling of your baby's silky skin under your fingers, while maintaining eye contact and chat while you massage – this will increase the sense of presence which in turn increases the relaxation for your baby and the secretion of happiness hormones, serotonin and oxytocin for both of you.

Presence in the moment or mindfulness can be trained. Initially, thoughts often wander while you are massaging and concentrating on the strokes. This is quite natural. When you notice this is happening, you just turn your attention back to what you are doing. Eventually, the mind will not wander as often as before, and you will feel more present, also because the strokes become second nature to you. Here are some exercises to train presence during massage:

Let the oil be lukewarm in your hands before your fingertips wander over his soft body. Notice your breathing and observe your baby's chest moving up and down. Let the feeling of his heart reach through the skin to your fingers. Stroke his head while gazing into his eyes, and notice his eyes searching to connect with yours. Let your movements across his body be soft and sensitive. Look at and feel your fingers. Look at his toes. Notice how fully present he is in the moment and how much he is enjoying this moment with you. Enjoy the moment equally by being present. Each time your mind wanders off, just accept that it has happened, and return to what you were doing.

> Being deeply loved by someone gives you strength, while loving someone deeply gives you courage.
>
> *Lao Tzu*

There are many opportunities to practice being present when interacting with your baby other than during baby massage.

Be present while you are feeding your baby, either from your breast or a bottle – avoid reading a book or magazine, watching TV or checking your mail. Observe his breathing, his sounds, and watch his face as he is enjoying himself eating. Try not to think about your later plans. Just be present. Be in the moment. Listen to his happy little slurps and feel the happiness this little person gives you. If your mind wanders elsewhere, just accept that it has happened and connect back to yourself and your baby. Breathe together. You share the same air.

Be present when you are out walking. Place your baby in the carrier or wrap close to your body and go for a short walk. Feel his movements on your skin like he is feeling your movements. Listen to his sounds, stroke his hair and cheeks and hold hands as you walk. If he is sleeping, you can focus fully on your own body. Let the mindful feeling saturate your whole being down to your legs and feet. Notice every step. Try to feel the whole sole of the foot against the ground. Maybe you can take off your shoes and walk barefoot on the grass and feel the grass between your toes. Notice all the movements under your feet. Practice walking slowly, and feel your feet roll from heel to toe, step by step.

Be present when you observe him, when he turns, rolls around, and explores the world. He explores life with curiosity. Lie down with him and explore with him. Even if you think you've seen that Lego he is exploring before, you have not seen exactly *that* Lego in *this* moment before. Touch it. Let your fingers be curious, let them explore. Maybe you should taste it a little. Maybe it has a sound. Perhaps it can be slammed against the brick he is holding in his hand.

> Being present together increases the experience.
> Take a moment to notice the:
>
> - Water flowing
> - Wind blowing
> - Flower blooming
> - Cars driving
> - People smiling
> - Dogs passing by waiving tales

Be present when you eat. Are you able to notice and enjoy every bite? Or are you just swallowing food while you are busy with other things? In this respect, we have a lot to learn from our babies. They are present in the moment. They really taste what they have in their mouth. They study each bite carefully. If they don't like it, it will come right back out. What they enjoy will induce big smiles and a clear desire for more. Notice your food while you eat. Savor each bite, one by one. Feel the flavors spreading in your mouth. It is so easy to throw a handful of blueberries into your mouth and even swallow without chewing properly. What's left is a slight taste, a filling of the stomach, not much else. Notice how the baby explores the food in front of him. How blueberries are carefully considered, one by one, before disappearing into the mouth. Let yourself be inspired by his way of eating. Let the flavors fill your mouth, be present while you are eating.

I love this poem. I keep it on my desk to remind me that every moment with my children are precious.

Imagine all those tiny seconds
you give me
a breath of time
little friend
every moment is a celebration of life
that will never
come again

But collect them I will
every single one
and gather them
like pearls on a string
so that I can recall
them again
that day my sweet little thing
is big

Unknown

Trust yourself; you are the best parent for your child.

Thank you,

To my loveable children, dear husband, loving parents, supportive brother and sister-in law, cherished family, good friends, inspirational colleagues, motivating and contributory teachers, sweet and trusting patients of all ages and the delightful, fun babies pictured in this book, constructive proof readers, translator, editors, fan and supporters, my readers.

Without you there would be no book.

Grateful and humble,

Dr. Kristin

Printed in the United States
By Bookmasters